PRAYING THE AGPIA

In loving memory of the

Very Rev. Fr Macarius Wahba

(1961 – 2020)

PRAYING THE
AGPIA

THE PRAYERS OF THE HOURS

H.H. POPE SHENOUDA III

ST SHENOUDA'S PRESS
SYDNEY, AUSTRALIA
2021

Praying the Agpia
H.H. Pope Shenoda III

COPYRIGHT © 2021
St Shenouda Press

All rights reserved. Except for brief quotations in critical publications or reviews, no part of this book may be reproduced in any manner without prior written permission from the publisher.

ST SHENOUDA PRESS
8419 Putty Rd,
Putty, NSW, 2330

www.stshenoudapress.com

ISBN 13: 978-0-6451394-0-2

All scripture quotations, unless otherwise indicated, are taken from the New King James Version®. Copyright © 1982 by Thomas Nelson, Inc. Used by permission. All rights reserved.

Contents

Why Do We Pray With The Agpia?	9
Aspects of Praying With the Agpia	19
The Agpia is a Biblical Teaching and a United Way of Prayer	31
The Life of Gladness and Joy in the Prayers of the Hours	39
The Agpia Prayers are a Love Song	45
In the Agpia there are Prayers and their Answers	53
Gladness and Rejoicing in the Agpia Prayers	61
In the Agpia Prayers, we get Reassurance about God's Promises, so we Become Glad	65
In the Agpia, there is Complete Reliance on God	75
The Agpia is a School of Faith	79
In the Agpia, there is Thanksgiving and Gratitude	87
Praises in the Agpia	95
Salvation in the Agpia Prayers	103
The Agpia, Knowing the Way, and our Spiritualities are Gifts of God	113

Preface

The story of this book started more than 20 years ago, when one of the Plymouth published a book criticizing the Agpia. So, we had a conference in Alexandria in 1976 and, as a result, published an article in Al-Keraza magazine entitled "Spirituality of the Agpia". Many others followed this article.

Prayers of the Agpia mean prayers of the hour. The name Agpia was derived from the word "Agp" in Coptic, meaning an hour.

There are Seven Prayers in the Agpia, that of the First, Third, Sixth, Ninth, Eleventh, and Twelfth Hour, as well as the Midnight Prayer. David the prophet referred to it in the great psalm saying "seven times a day I praise you, because of your righteous judgments" (Ps 119:164).

The prayers of the Agpia contain a general introduction, Psalms, requests, some passages, prayers common to all hours, an absolution, and a general conclusion to every prayer.

In this book, we explain the many spiritual benefits of praying with the Agpia. Furthermore, we explain the evidence regarding this type of praying and its use in the apostolic times. Also discussed, is the use of Psalms since the old days of our apostolic fathers.

Praying with the Agpia has several aspects of prayer. It teaches us how to converse with God; it contains supplication, gladness, joy, glorification, thanksgiving, and submission to God. It also includes the orthodox doctrine in detail, and reminds us of important events that must be kept in our minds all the time.

It is a school in prayer, teaching you how to pray. If you pray with it, remember me before God and pray for me.

Pope Shenouda III

July 1998

Translated September 1999 By K.G.

Why Do We Pray With The Agpia?

We pray with it because of its spirituality and ideality, and for many reasons including;

1. It extends the time spent with God

A person may stand to pray saying only a few words and that would be it; s/he does not find anything else to say. However, a worshipper using the Agpia will find a lot of material to pray with. It is going to make her/him stand before God for a quarter of an hour or more if s/he wants. In this regard, we can also say that,

2. The Agpia is a school teaching you to pray

We need to learn how to pray. Even the Lord's disciples asked Him saying, "Lord, teach us to pray..." (Luke 11:1). With the Agpia we learn what to say in our prayers, and what the appropriate manner used to converse with God is; we train our tongue and heart to talk with God.

3. The Agpia contains all types of prayers

A person praying without the Agpia may remember some requests and then concludes her/his prayer. However, with the Agpia s/he realizes that there are types of prayers; the request, thanksgiving, humility, a broken heart, confession, and repentance. The Agpia also contains prayers of glorifying and praising God, prayers of love, and contemplating His beautiful characteristics.

For example, when you say "Holy, Holy, Holy is the Lord of hosts. Heaven and earth are full of Your glory and honor..." you are not requesting anything. Furthermore, this is neither a thanksgiving nor a repentance prayer; but rather for glorifying God and contemplating His holiness and might...

Furthermore, when you conclude your Agpia prayers with "O Christ, our good Lord, plenteous in patience, mercy and compassion, who loves the just and shows mercy to all sinners..." you are contemplating the beautiful characteristics of God.

4. Hence, the Agpia teaches us how to praise

It teaches us to glorify and contemplate on the beautiful characteristics of God. This is why many Psalms have the phrase "Praise the Lord!", "Praise the Lord! Praise, O servants of the Lord", "Oh, sing to the Lord a new song", "Praise the Lord, O Jerusalem!". What does this praise mean? How should it be? We learn this from the Agpia prayers.

5. We also pray with the Agpia because it contains a lot of details

Who among us, when praying for the forgiveness of her/his sins, prays for the forgiveness of sins which s/he committed willingly and unwillingly, knowingly and unknowingly, the hidden and the visible?! We remember all of those in our Agpia prayers.

Why Do We Pray With The Agpia?

Who among us, when giving thanks to God in her/his own prayers, gives thanks as in the Agpia " for He has protected, assisted, preserved and accepted us, had compassion upon us, supported us and brought us to this hour"?!

Who among us remembers all of the details that we say in the Agpia in the conclusion of every prayer "Sanctify our souls, purify our bodies, set right our thoughts, cleanse our intentions, heal our sickness, forgive us our sins and deliver us from every evil grief and distress. Surround us with your holy angels that we may be guided and guarded with them...". Who among us remembers, in her/his own prayer, to ask for being surrounded by His holy angels to be guarded and guided with them? We remember this in the Agpia prayers.

It teaches us prayer and accuracy so that God gets involved in everything in our lives

The content of the details of the Agpia prayers is very long, and has many examples. In summary, it teaches us prayer and accuracy so that God gets involved in everything in our lives. We do not leave out anything without talking to Him about it.

6. The Agpia contains prayers that are according to God's will, hence its ideality

Many times our prayers are not answered, because they were not according to God's will; this is why we say in the Lord's prayer "Thy will be done...". The Agpia prayers are all according to God's will because most of them are with Psalms which were said by the Holy Spirit through David (Mat. 22:43). These Psalms are part of the Bible. Therefore, in our prayers with the Psalms we talk to God with His own words that were inspired to David by the Holy Spirit. Thus, we ensure that our prayers are answered.

The saints put the rest of the prayers forth, and everything in them is in agreement with the spirit of the Bible.

7. Reminding us of important holy events also contributes to the Agpia's ideality

We may not remember these events in our daily lives if praying without the Agpia.

> * In the Morning Prayer, we remember the incarnation of the Lord and His eternity. We also acknowledge that He is the true light and we ask Him to enlighten us.
>
> * In the Prayer of the Third Hour, we remember the hour when the Holy Spirit came down on the disciples and we ask Him to work in us.
>
> * In the Prayer of the Sixth Hour, we remember the crucifixion of the Lord for our sake and what that means in terms of His feelings towards us.
>
> * In the Prayer of the Ninth Hour, We remember the confession of the right thief and the death of the Lord for our sake.
>
> * In the Sunset Prayer, we remember those who came to the Lord at the end of the day, at eleven O'clock.
>
> * In the Prayer of the Twelfth Hour, we remember death, the end of the world, the judgement day, and the need to be prepared for it.
>
> * In the Midnight Prayer, we remember the second coming of the Lord and what that requires of watching, repentance, and tears...

Why Do We Pray With The Agpia?

Who among us remembers all of these events, and enjoys their spiritual effects, if praying without the Agpia?!

No doubt that all of these events, which we remember everyday through our prayers with the Agpia, become focused in our minds and become part of our feelings and beliefs. They have a firm effect on our spirits; which becomes evident in our daily lives and manners.

8. We pray with the Agpia because it keeps our minds always focused on God

We pray every three hours with the Agpia; thus, we lift our hearts to God all the time, day and night. Our thoughts, hearts, and tongues would not stop being directed towards God. Therefore, through the Agpia we follow God's commandment that says "men always ought to pray and not lose heart..." (Luke 18:1), and that which says "pray without ceasing..." (1 Thessalonians 5:17).

Doing this is easy: by memorizing the Agpia prayers, and praying it without the book through the hours of the day. You can lift your heart to God and pray, even for a few minutes, with no one else realizing that you are praying. The important thing is that we stay in the presence of God.

9. Preoccupying your mind with God in this way allows your thoughts to be humble

As a result of being influenced by the words of your continuous prayers, your mind will be embarrassed of thinking about sins or trivial matters. Even during the time when you are not praying, these words will be in the back of your mind resisting all evil. On the other hand, they will be a source of contemplations.

10. The Agpia is also ideal because it contains the preaching and teaching aspect

For example, the Morning Prayer includes a passage from the Epistle of St. Paul to the Ephesians that says "I, therefore, the prisoner of the Lord, beseech you to lead a life worthy of the calling with which you were called, with all lowliness and gentleness, with long-suffering, bearing with one another in love, endeavoring to keep the unity of the Spirit in the bond of peace...", (Eph. 4:1-3). This is a spiritual plan that outlines your behavior throughout the day.

At the same time, this Prayer offers us the Psalm which gives spiritual advice on how to behave all day " Blessed is the man who walks not in the counsel of the ungodly, nor stands in the path of sinners, nor sits on the seat of the scornful; but his delight is in the law of the Lord, and in His law he meditates day and night...". When the worshipper remembers the words of this Psalm, these words become like a sermon throughout the day.

Then the worshipper reads in Psalm 15(14) " Lord, who may abide in your tabernacle? Who may dwell in your holy hill? He who walks uprightly, and works righteousness, and speaks the truth in his heart; he who does not backbite with his tongue, nor does evil to his neighbor, nor does he take up a reproach against his friend...". This is another sermon that the worshipper says to her/himself when praying; s/he always reminds her/himself of it.

In the Prayer of the Third Hour, the worshipper comes across another sermon in Psalm 24 (23), where it says "Who may ascend into the hill of the Lord? Or who may stand in his holy place? He who has clean hands and a pure heart, who has not lifted up his soul to an idol, nor sworn deceitfully...".

Why Do We Pray With The Agpia?

In the Prayer of the Sixth Hour, the worshipper encounters the "blessings" and a part of the Sermon on the mountain, then concludes the Psalms with the phrase "holiness adorns Your house, O Lord..."

In the Prayer of the Ninth Hour, there is another sermon in the Psalm "I will sing of mercy..." as it says, "I will walk within my house with a perfect heart. I will set nothing wicked before my eyes...A perverse heart shall depart from me...Whoever secretly slanders his neighbor, him I will destroy..." (Ps.101(100)). Even if the worshipper does not do what is described in the Psalm, it will, at least, remind her/him of the right thing to do.

In the Sunset Prayer, we find many sermons: "this is the gate of the Lord, through which the righteous shall enter..." (Ps. 118(117)), "I was glad when they said to me: let us go into the house of the Lord..." (Ps. 122(121)), "unless the Lord builds the house, they labor in vain who build it..." (Ps. 127(126))

Furthermore, in the Prayer of the Twelfth Hour, we find a lesson about humility in His saying in Psalm 131(130) " Lord, my heart is not haughty, nor my eyes lofty. Neither do I concern myself with great matters, nor with things that are too profound for me...". There are also lessons in serving God, in David's saying "surely I will not go into the chamber of the house, or go up to the comfort of my bed; I will not give sleep to my eyes or slumber to my eyelids, until I find a place for the Lord, a dwelling-place for the mighty God of Jacob..." (Ps. 132(131)). Another lesson in praying "all you servants of the Lord, who by the night stand in the house of the Lord! Lift up your hands in the sanctuary, and bless the Lord..." (Ps 134(133)).

Also, in the Midnight Prayer, we find a great example, in the Great Psalm (Ps.119(118)), regarding the relationship with God's words, commandments, and testimonies in "how sweet are Your words to my taste, sweeter than honey to my mouth...", "Your word is a lamp to my feet and a light to my path...".

11. Another reason for the ideality of the Agpia is that it teaches us to remember God's words and the biblical verses

Every Prayer includes a chapter from the gospel. Thus, whoever gets used to praying with the Agpia will find her/himself remembering several chapters from the gospel of the day's Hours and also the three services of the Midnight Prayer. Furthermore, s/he will remember the verses of the Psalms that s/he repeats; these are many.

Consequently, you find that whoever keeps praying with the Agpia will be remembering a lot of written passages and a lot of verses from not only the gospel but also from the Psalms. These will be used in her/his daily life, and would have a great influence on the person's feelings.

12. We pray from the Agpia because it unites all members of the church in a single prayer

The same prayers are being said by all members of the church, in all the See of St. Mark: in Egypt, Sudan, Jerusalem, and all countries of the East. The same prayers are used in the U.S., Canada, Europe, Australia, and Africa. All are praying with one spirit and one mind so that they feel the holy life of fellowship. This occurs in the same way as when they pray the Eucharist, and all other Sacraments, during a common mass using the same Liturgy.

13. These same Prayers also unite the hearts and feelings of worshippers

They even help in the unity of spirituality by uniting the terms used in prayers, sermons and spiritual teachings that are contained in the Agpia. These Prayers also aid in uniting the contemplations, feelings and the effects of those terms on these feelings.

In this way, we become one church, not only in the doctrine and rituals but also in spirituality. We will never attain this unity if every one prays her/his own way.

14. We pray from the Agpia because this was the ideal prayer that our saintly fathers used

In this way, we protect our holy traditions, and become not only one church in terms of doctrine, rituals, and spirituality during our own generation but also for all generations. By the grace of God, we will discuss this issue in more detail later on.

15. Also from its ideality, the Agpia deepens the doctrines of faith in our inner selves

In every Prayer, we say the Creed of faith so that its teachings are deepened in us; we also obtain spiritual feelings from it. Furthermore, we mention the Holy Trinity in the Trisagion. We also mention the divinity, incarnation, and ever existence of the Son. We mention His crucifixion and death in the Prayers of the Sixth and Ninth Hours. And we mention His Second Coming in the Midnight Prayer.

We mention the Holy Spirit in the Prayer of the Third Hour.

We mention the ever-virginity of St. Mary in more than one place.

We will also find so many names and characteristics of God in the Agpia.

Moreover, praying with the Agpia allows us to form relationships with angels and saints.

16. One important use of the Agpia is that it organizes our prayers

It reminds us of their times and invites us to pray so that we feel guilty if we did not pray at a time that should have been devoted to prayer. In contrast, if we have our own way and freedom in praying, we might neglect prayers and lose their regular basis.

17. Praying with the Agpia is full of all kinds of emotions

The Agpia is a prayer of love, faith, submission, consolation, gladness, and joy. Each one of these points needs to be more elaborated on.

Aspects of Praying With the Agpia

Praying with the Agpia has many aspects from which we learn to pray. If we pray just by improvisation our prayers may not contain these aspects.

What are these aspects?

1. A Conversation with God

Prayer, as it may seem to some, is just talking to God. But this talk in the Agpia has many aspects. There is love, eagerness, praise, glorification, and contemplating the beautiful characteristics of God, as was mentioned previously.

The Agpia Prayer also has other aspects: submission, kneeling, and conversing in an attempt to persuade God that your request is for good; you present your case with honesty. It also contains crying out for help, asking for guidance, for knowledge, for learning, and thanksgiving by recalling God's grace on the worshiper. There is also asking for mercy, God's justice, submitting one's life to God, waiting for the Lord, and relying on Him with hope. In the Agpia, there is gladness, peace, talking about the

2. Submission

Praying with the Agpia teaches us to submit to God and to start the Prayer with kneeling. We emphasize this so that people who pray while sitting down or those who stand up with no respect to God may get embarrassed. Praying with the Agpia teaches us to start the Prayer of the First Hour with "O' come, let us worship; O' come, let us ask Christ our God. O' come, let us worship; O' come, let us ask Christ our King. O' come, let us worship; O' come, let us ask Christ our Savior". So we repeat the phrase O' come, let us worship three times. (In Arabic, the verb worship includes the act of kneeling in addition to adoration, Translation Note).

The phrases that indicate worshiping are many in the Psalms we pray with. In the Prayer of the First Hour, we say in Psalm 5 "I will come into Your house in the multitude of Your mercy; in fear I will worship toward Your holy temple".

In the Prayer of the Ninth Hour, we say in Psalm 96(95) "Give to the Lord glory and strength. Give to the Lord the glory due His name; bring an offering, and come to His courts. Oh, worship the Lord in the beauty of holiness! Tremble before Him, all the earth". And in Psalm 97(96), we say "Worship Him, all you gods". Furthermore, we say in Psalm 99(98) "Exalt the Lord our God, and worship at His footstool; for He is holy. Exalt the Lord our God, and worship at His holy hill; for the Lord our God is holy". And in Psalm 111(110) "Holy and awesome is His name. The fear of the Lord is the beginning of wisdom". Moreover, the worshipper says submissively, in the Great Psalm, "Let my cry come before You, O Lord; give me understanding

Aspects of Praying With the Agpia

according to Your word. Let my supplication come before You; deliver me according to You word" (Ps. 119(118)).

Submission before God is a biblical teaching that is applied by the Agpia.

In Revelation "the twenty-four elders fall down before him who sits on the throne and worship him who lives forever and ever, and cast their crowns before the throne, saying: "You are worthy, O Lord, to receive glory and honor and power" (Rev. 4:10,11). This falling down and worshipping by the elders and the four beasts is repeated in Rev. 5:14.

St John heard the victorious people praising "Who shall not fear you, O Lord, and glorify your name? For you alone are holy. For all nations shall come and worship before you, for your judgements have been manifested" (Rev. 15:4).

A worshipper praying with the Agpia talks with God as if talking to his father

3. **Conversation**

Despite this submission before God, a worshipper praying with the Agpia talks with God as if talking to his father.

Such a worshipper will say in the Morning Prayer "Do not enter into judgement with Your servant, for in Your sight no one living is righteous" (Psalm 143(142)). S/he repeats the same meaning in Psalm 130(129) of the Prayer of the Twelfth Hour saying "If You, Lord, should mark iniquities, O Lord, who could stand? But there is forgiveness with you". S/he also says in the Morning Prayer "Who can understand his errors? Cleanse me from secret faults" (Ps. 19(18)); and in Psalm 25(24) "Remember, O Lord, Your tender mercies and Your loving kindness, for they have been from of old. Do not remember the sins of my youth nor my transgressions... according to Your mercy and not to our sins".

It is also said in Psalm 3 "Lord, how they have increased who trouble me"; and in Psalm 13(12) "How long, O Lord? Will You forget me forever?". The Lord says in Psalm 25(24) "Consider my enemies, for they are many; and they hate me with cruel hatred. Oh, keep my soul, and deliver me..."; and in Psalm 13(12) He says "Enlighten my eyes, lest I sleep the sleep of the death; lest my enemy say, "I have prevailed against him". Furthermore, in Psalm 30(29) of the Prayer of the Third Hour, the Lord explains saying "What profit is there in my blood, when I go to the pit? Will the dust praise You? Will it declare Your truth?".

4. Honesty

A worshipper praying from the Agpia presents her/his case very honestly speaking about her/his weaknesses, the prevailing of her/his enemy, and the inability s/he has in saving her/himself.

Therefore, the worshipper says in Psalm 143(142), from the Morning Prayer, "For the enemy has persecuted my soul; he has crushed my life to the ground; he has made me dwell in the darkness, like those who have long been dead". In Psalm 3, s/he says, "Many are they who rise up against me. Many are they who say of me, "There is no help for him in God"; and in Psalm 41(40), from the Prayer of the Third Hour, "My enemies speak evil of me: "When will he die, and his name perish?". Moreover, the worshipper says in Psalm 142(141), from the Prayer of the Twelfth Hour, "Then You knew my path. In the way in which I walk they have secretly set a snare for me. Look on my right hand and see, for there is no one who acknowledges me; refuge has failed me; no one cares for my soul. I cried out to You, O Lord".

Aspects of Praying With the Agpia

5. Crying out for help

When praying with the Psalms of the Agpia, the worshipper cries out for help from God.

In Psalm 70(69), from the Prayer of the First and Sixth Hours, the worshipper prays "Make haste, O God, to deliver me! Make haste to help me, O Lord! You are my help and deliverer; O Lord, do not delay". Also in Psalm 86(85), from the Prayer of the Sixth Hour, "Be merciful to me, O Lord, for I cry to You all day long. Rejoice the soul of Your servant, for to You, O Lord, I lift up my soul... for You are abundant in mercy to all those who call upon You". In the Prayer of the Twelfth Hour, the worshipper says in Psalm 130(129) "Out of the depths I have cried to You, O Lord; Lord, hear my voice"; and in Psalm 141(140) "Lord, I cry out to You; make haste to me! Give ear to my voice when I cry out to You". And in Psalm 142(141) "I cry out to the Lord with my voice; with my voice to the Lord I make my supplication. I pour out my complaint before Him; I declare before Him my trouble. When my spirit was overwhelmed within me, then You knew my path".

We say this because some people's prayers have no emotions or spirit; they do not cry out to the Lord or beg Him...

6. Guidance

The worshipper who prays from the Agpia always asks for the Lord's guidance. S/he asks Him to let her/him know the right way to take, His commandments, His justice, and His judgements...

In the Morning Prayer, such a worshipper will say "Teach me to do Your will, for You are my God; Your Spirit is good. Lead me in the land of the upright". In Psalm 27(26), s/he also says " "Teach me Your way, O Lord, and lead me in a smooth path..."; and in Psalm 25(24) "Show me Your ways,

O Lord; teach me Your paths. Lead me in Your truth and teach me", and then the worshipper says about the Lord "The humble He teaches His way".

In Psalm 5 the worshipper says "Lead me, O Lord, in Your righteousness... make Your way straight before my face". Also in Psalm 23(22), of the Prayer of the Third Hour, "The Lord is my shepherd...He leads me in the paths of righteousness For His name's sake". Furthermore, the worshipper says in Psalm 86(85) of the Prayer of the Sixth Hour "Teach me Your way, O Lord; I will walk in Your truth".

In the passage "Lord, by Your grace..." of the Prayer of the Twelfth Hour, the worshipper says "Blessed are You, Lord, teach me Your justice, show me Your will, enlighten me to Your goodness...Teach me to do Your will".

In the Midnight Prayer, the Great Psalm 119(118), the worshipper says "Teach me Your statutes"; "Open my eyes, that I may see wondrous things from Your law. I am a stranger in the earth; do not hide Your commandments from me"; " Teach me, O Lord, the way of the statutes, and I shall keep it to the end"; "Give me understanding, that I may learn Your commandments"; "Accept, I pray, the freewill offering of my mouth, O Lord, and teach me Your judgements"; "I am Your servant; give me understanding, that I may know Your testimonies"; "Make Your face shine upon Your servant, and teach me Your statutes"; and "Give me understanding, and I shall live"...

In the passage "Have mercy upon us O God, have mercy upon us...", at the end of every Prayer, the worshipper says "Ease our lives, and guide us to act according to Your commandments". It is really good that the worshipper asks for the guidance of the Lord in order to know how to act according to His commandments. Here we remember

Aspects of Praying With the Agpia

how the apostles asked the Lord saying "Lord, teach us to pray" (Luke 11:1).

7. Asking for mercy

In every Prayer of the Agpia, we say Psalm 51(50) which starts with "Have mercy upon me, O God". In the Morning Prayer, the worshiper says in Psalm 6 "Have mercy on me, O Lord, for I am weak; O Lord, heal me, for my bones are troubled. My soul is also troubled; but You, O Lord, how long? Return, O Lord, deliver me! Oh, save me for Your mercies' sake...O Lord, do not rebuke me in Your anger, nor chasten me in Your hot displeasure". Also, in Psalm 27(26), the worshipper says "Do not turn Your servant away in anger...do not leave me nor forsake me, O God of my salvation...do not deliver me to the will of my adversaries".

In every Prayer of the Agpia, we repeat the phrase "Lord, have mercy" (Kir-ye ley-son) for 41 times, asking for God's mercy. We ask for mercy a lot when we pray from the Agpia. This might remind us with the prayer of tax collector "God be merciful to me a sinner"..."this man went down to his house justified" (Luke 18:13,14).

8. Reliance on God

It is part of our prayer to declare our reliance on God in everything, and this brings us happiness. The worshipper says in the Morning Prayer "To You, O Lord I lift up my soul. O my God, I trust in You; let me not be ashamed; let not my enemies triumph over me...let me not be ashamed for I put my trust in You".

Furthermore, the worshipper says in Psalm 16(15) "Preserve me, O God, for in You I put my trust".; and in Psalm 5 "But let all those rejoice who put

> *It is part of our prayer to declare our reliance on God in everything, and this brings us happiness*

their trust in You; let them ever shout for joy, because You defend them".

9. Waiting for the Lord

The Agpia teaches us to ask and not be anxious, but rather to wait for the Lord.

In Psalm 25(24) of the Morning Prayer, the worshipper says "On You I wait all the day", "Indeed, let no one who waits on You be ashamed", "Let integrity and uprightness preserve me, for I wait for You". The Agpia also teaches us to wait for the Lord in hope, and with a strong and confident heart; the worshipper says in Psalm 27(26) "Wait on the Lord,; be of good courage, and he shall strengthen Your heart; wait, I say, on the Lord". Furthermore, in Psalm 130(129) of the Prayer of the Twelfth Hour, the worshipper prays "I wait for the Lord, my soul waits, and in His word I do hope. My soul waits for the Lord more than those who watch for the morning...".

10. The relationship with God

The worshipper says, in Psalm 27(26) of the Morning Prayer, "When my father and my mother forsake me, then the Lord will take care of me". The most important thing in the relationship with God is that the worshipper asks for God Himself, saying in the same Psalm, "When You said: Seek My face, my heart said to You: Your face, Lord , I will seek. Do not hide Your face from me".

S/he says "One thing I have desired of the Lord, that will I seek: that I may dwell in the in the house of the Lord all the days of my life, to behold the beauty of the Lord, and to inquire in His temple".

People cry out saying "Oh, taste and see that the Lord is good" (Ps. 34(33), of the Prayer of the Third Hour). The worshipper talks about her/his relationship with God "I will bless the Lord at all times; His praise shall continually be in my mouth. My soul shall make its boast in the Lord" (Ps. 34(33)).

11. Thanksgiving

The worshipper who prays with the Agpia always remembers God's grace on her/him. S/he always remembers God answering her/his prayers and requests: the worshipper says in Psalm 4 of the Morning Prayer "Hear me when I call, O God of my righteousness! You have delivered me when I was in distress...The Lord will hear when I call to Him". Also s/he says in Psalm 118(117) of the Sunset Prayer "I will praise You, for You have answered me, and have become my salvation". Moreover, in Psalm 119(118) of the Midnight Prayer, the worshipper says "I cry out with my whole heart; hear me, O Lord".

Do we always in our own prayers, as compared to the Agpia Prayers, thank God for answering our prayers?! Or do we ask, and when being answered we become happy forgetting to give thanks?!

The worshipper who prays from the Agpia remembers the gifts of God. S/he will say "But know that the Lord has set apart for Himself him who is godly...You have put gladness in my heart...I will both lie down in peace, and sleep; for You alone, O Lord, make me dwell in safety" (Ps. 4, Morning Prayer). Also, in Psalm 27(26) of the Morning Prayer s/he prays "For in the time of trouble He shall hide me in His pavilion; in the secret place of His tabernacle He shall hide me; He shall set me high upon a rock. And now my head shall be lifted up above my enemies all around me; therefore I will offer sacrifices of joy in His tabernacle; I will sing, yes, I will sing praises to the Lord"

In the Sunset Prayer, Psalm 118(117), the worshipper says "The right hand of the Lord does valiantly. I shall not die, but live"; and "Oh, give thanks to the Lord, for He is good! For His mercy endures forever".

The worshipper sings joyfully because s/he is rescued by God, saying in the Sunset Prayer: "If it had not been the Lord who was on our side, when men rose up against us, then they would have swallowed us alive...Our soul has escaped as a bird from the snare of the fowlers; the snare is broken, and we have escaped. Our help is in the name of the Lord, who made heaven and earth" (Ps. 124(123)). S/he says to the Lord in the Prayer of the Twelfth Hour, Psalm 138(137), "You will stretch out Your hand against the wrath of my enemies, and Your right hand will save me. The Lord will perfect that which concerns me; Your mercy, O Lord, endures forever; do not forsake the works of Your hands".

> *The worshipper sings joyfully because he is rescued by God*

12. Gladness and peace

As you find tears in the Agpia, you also find gladness.

An example of that is in the Sunset Prayer; almost all of Psalm 126(125) is about gladness as the worshipper says "We were like those who dream. Then our mouth was filled with laughter, and our tongue with singing. Then they said among the nations, "The Lord has done great things for us", The Lord has done great things for us, whereof we are glad...Those who sow in tears shall reap in joy".

The worshipper also says in Psalm 67(66) of the Morning Prayer and the Prayer of the Sixth Hour "Oh, let the nations be glad and sing for joy! For You shall judge the people righteously, and govern the nations on earth. Let the peoples praise You, O God; let all the peoples praise

Aspects of Praying With the Agpia

You. Then the earth shall yield her increase; God, our own God, shall bless us".

Furthermore, in Psalm 56 of the Prayer of the Sixth Hour, the worshipper rejoices with salvation in a lot of details; s/he praises God with a lute and a harp.

13. Asking for salvation

One of the most important things we ask for is to be saved.

It is a request that is repeated a lot in the Agpia. The worshipper prays in Psalm 12(11) of the Morning Prayer "Help, Lord, for the godly man ceases...You shall preserve them from this generation forever". And in the Prayer of the Sixth Hour, s/he says "Save me, O God, by Your name" (Ps. 54(53)), "Show us Your mercy, O Lord, and grant us Your salvation" (Ps. 85(84)); almost all of the latter Psalm is about salvation.

In the Midnight Prayer, the worshipper says in the Great Psalm, Psalm 119(118), "I am Yours, save me", and "My eyes fail from seeking Your salvation".

14. A lot of requests

The worshipper not only asks for God's mercy, but also His justice.

S/he says in Psalm 5 of the Morning Prayer "Lead me, O Lord, in Your righteousness because of my enemies; Make Your ways straight before my face". S/he also says in Psalm 143(142) of the Morning Prayer "In Your faithfulness answer me, and in Your righteousness". (In the Arabic version, the noun righteousness is replaced by justice, Translation Note).

Therefore, God's justice considers the human nature and the powers of the attacking enemies; God's justice is merciful on man.

> *God's justice is merciful on man*

As a consequence, the worshipper who uses the Agpia asks for God's support, saying in Psalm 54(53) of the Prayer of the Sixth Hour "Hear my prayer, O God; give ear to the word of my mouth. For strangers have risen up against me, and oppressors have sought after my life; they did not set God before them". Also in the Prayer of the Third Hour, the worshipper says "Vindicate me, O God...For You are the God of my strength" (Ps. 43(42)).

The number of requests found in the passage "Have mercy upon us O God...", at the end of each Prayer, is very large.

These are requests that no one would remember if praying without the Agpia. This is because the worshipper says "ease our lives, and guide us to act according to Your commandments. Sanctify our souls, purify our bodies, set right our thoughts, cleanse our intentions, heal our sickness, forgive us our sins and deliver us from every evil grief and distress. Surround us with Your Holy angels that we may be guided and guarded with them...".

15. The Agpia and Faith

Our holy church does not separate our prayers from Faith.

We believe in God, so we converse with Him in our Prayers. We mention this faith in great detail in the Agpia, so that the worshipper deepens her/his faith in God.

The Agpia is a Biblical Teaching and a United Way of Prayer

* The church prayed with Psalms in the Old and New Testaments

* The apostolic fathers used to pray the Prayers of the Hours

* Praying with the Agpia does not eliminate your own prayer in addition to the Agpia

* The church has wisdom in putting forth the Prayers of the Hours

SPECIFYING HOLY TIMES

Some people ask questions about the Agpia, including;

Are not all times holy? Why, then, specify particular times but not others?

Doesn't the bible ask us to pray at all times (Luke 18:1)?

In fact, the first to specify holy times was God Himself. Although our entire lives are with God and all our days are for Him, God- glory be to His name- specified one holy day in the week, called the Day of the Lord. Our Lord said about that day "Remember the Sabbath day, to keep it holy...but the seventh day is the Sabbath of the Lord your God" (Ex. 20:8,10) (Duet. 5:12).

The Lord specified one day per week to be devoted to Him, as a minimum requirement. Whoever wishes to devote more than that can, without objection, do so. This is the same with the Prayers of the Hours.

This is not only in the Old Testament, but also in the New Testament. St. John the apostle says in Revelation "I was in the spirit in the Lord's day" (Rev. 1:10). Saturday was changed to Sunday, but specifying one day for the Lord is the same...for God is the same, yesterday, today, and forever (Heb. 13:8).

In Leviticus, there is a list through which God says "These are the feasts of the Lord, holy convocations which you shall proclaim at their appointed times" (Lev. 23:4). This list contained the Sabbath, the Passover, the Feast of the First Fruits, the Feast of Weeks, and others. In the New Testament, the Passover became a truth instead of only a symbol (1 Cor. 5:7). The Feast of the First Fruits became Feast of Holy Resurrection after decoding the symbol. The Feast of the Weeks became the Pentecost in exactly the same time.

Some details were changed, but the Godly teaching remained the same without any change; I mean specifying holy times for God.

The Bible says "For Moses has had throughout many generations those who preach him in every city, being read in the synagogues every Sabbath" (Acts 15:21). The essence is still present, reading the Holy Bible changed from the Books of Moses and the prophets to the Gospel and Epistles; also the Sabbath is now Sunday. Thus, the principle is still there, because the Lord Christ was asked to read Isaiah on the Sabbath, so He read it; He did not order that to be stopped.

Therefore, specifying times for an organized way of worshipping is a Divine and Biblical teaching.

Praying with memorized Prayers

In the New Testament, the disciples asked the Lord saying, "Lord, teach us to pray", so He said to them "When You pray, say: Our Father in Heaven…" (Luke 11:1-4). From that time, the principle of praying with a memorized prayer was established as He taught His disciples to repeat a prayer that they memorized from Him.

Praying with Psalms

In the Old Testament, Psalms were an important part of a memorized prayers principle; people used to pray with them. The Psalm that people used to sing while going up to the Sanctuary used to be called (The Psalms of Ascension).

Some people might say that Psalms were only restricted to the Old Testament! No, they are in the New Testament as well.

Our teacher St. Paul the Apostle says, "Whenever you come together, each of you has a psalm" (1Cor. 14:26). He also says "Speaking with one another in psalms and hymns and spiritual songs, singing and making melody in your heart to the Lord" (Eph. 5:19). "Let the word of Christ dwell in you richly in all wisdom, teaching and admonishing one another in psalms and hymns and spiritual songs, singing with grace in your hearts to the Lord" (Col. 3:16).

Therefore, praying with the Psalms and singing them is a Godly and Biblical teaching.

Psalms present us with a clear picture of the Lord Christ, so we remember Him when praying. The biggest two Books of the Old Testament that talked about the Lord Christ were Isaiah and Psalms. The Lord said, "All things must be fulfilled which were written in the Law of Moses and the Prophets and the Psalms concerning me" (Luke 24:44).

Therefore, we see the Lord and remember Him when we pray with the Agpia.

THE SEVEN PRAYERS ARE A BIBLICAL TEACHING

The question remains unanswered: are the seven Prayers a Biblical teaching?

Yes, the seven Prayers are a Biblical teaching. The Bible says "Seven times a day I praise You, because of Your righteous judgements" (Ps. 119:164).

Organization of the Prayers started with three: Vespers, Morning and Noon; that is, the beginning, the end and the middle of the day. This is as Daniel the Prophet prayed three times a day (Dan. 6:10). Then, Prayers were organized into the Hours of the day and the Hours of the night…Let us now discuss the times of the seven Prayers with the Bible being our reference.

The Morning Prayer is very obvious, it is a Biblical teaching.

The Bible says "God, You are my God; early I will seek You; my soul thirsts for You" (Ps. 63:1) "My voice You shall hear in the morning, O Lord; in the morning I will direct it to You, and I will look up" (Ps. 5:3). The Lord Himself says, "Those who seek me diligently will find me" (Pro. 8:17). (In the Arabic edition, the word diligently is in fact replaced

The Agpia is a Biblical Teaching and a United Way of Prayer

by early Translation Note). It is commonsense to start the day with prayers. This is the appropriate manner and is a commandment, for God must always be "In the beginning...".

As the day started with God, it should also end with God.

As the day started with God, it should also end with God.

If we were a sacrifice to God (Rev. 12:1) and if sacrifices are presented day and night, then we should offer Him the evening (night) sacrifice. The Bible says "Let my prayer be set before you as incense, the lifting up of my hands as the evening sacrifice" (Ps. 141:2). Thus, we say in the Absolution of the Sunset Prayer "Thank you, compassionate Lord, for You granted us to pass this day in peace, brought us thankfully to the night and made us worthy of seeing Your light until sunset".

We pray before going to bed at least to make our beds holy before we sleep. Thus, God will be the last thing we think of before sleep. The Psalmist said "Surely I will not go into the chamber of my house, or go up to the comfort of my bed; I will not give sleep to my eyes or slumber to my eyelids, until I find a place for the Lord, a dwelling place for the Mighty God of Jacob" (Ps. 132:3-5)...a dwelling place in my heart.

Therefore, praying before sleep (the Prayer of the Twelfth Hour) and all that is before this is a Biblical teaching.

The Midnight Prayer is also a Biblical teaching. God says, "By the night stand in the house of the Lord! Lift up your hands in the sanctuary, and bless the Lord" (Ps. 134:1,2). The Lord also advises us to watch and pray "Blessed are those servants whom the master, when he comes, will find them watching" (Luke 12:37). This is why the church considers it appropriate to pray every service of the four services of the night ending with the Morning Prayer.

THE MIDNIGHT PRAYER IS ALSO A BIBLICAL TEACHING

The singer says "At midnight I will rise to give thanks to you, because of your righteous judgements" (Ps. 119:64). The Bible also says "And at midnight a cry was heard: behold, the bridegroom is coming; go out to meet him" (Mat. 25:6). Thus, we watch praying in order to be ready to meet the bridegroom. The details of the Midnight Prayer is also a Biblical teaching.

God, Himself, says "Blessed are those servants whom the master, when he comes, will find them watching...And if he should come in the second watch, or come in the third watch, and finds them so, blessed are those servants" (Luke 12:37,38). There is no doubt that it is a spiritual church that teaches her children to watch in prayers, to be ready according to God's will.

> *It is a spiritual church that teaches her children to watch in prayers, to be ready according to God's will*

The details of the day's Prayers (Third, Sixth, and Ninth Hour) is also a Biblical teaching and an apostolic heritage. The saintly apostles prayed with these Prayers.

The Bible says "Peter went up on the housetop to pray, at about the sixth hour" (Acts 10:9). It also says "Now Peter and John went up together to the temple at the hour of prayer, the ninth hour" (Acts 3:1). We are not as wise or comprehending as our apostolic fathers who prayed at these two hours. Furthermore, the third hour, when the Holy Spirit came down on the disciples (Acts 2:15), was undoubtedly an hour of prayer.

The Agpia is a Biblical Teaching and a United Way of Prayer

Therefore, the seven Hours of prayer in the Agpia are a Biblical teaching, in general and in detail.

There are some remaining questions;

* What is the point of having such an organized way of prayer?

* What is the spiritual benefit for the worshipper and the church?

* Is it justified for the church to put forth an organized way of prayer? And is it possible for the church to have the power to influence the believer's conscience, the believer who is free to pray whenever and by whatever way s/he wants?

The Life of Gladness and Joy in the Prayers of the Hours

THE POWER OF THE CHURCH

Some people might ask, regarding the Prayers of the Hours;

Is it justified for the church to put forth an organized way of prayer?

Yes, the Lord Christ said to His apostles "Go therefore and make disciples of all the nations...teaching them to observe all things that I have commanded you" (Mat. 28:19). Thus, the first task of the church is teaching. This is why the apostles said "But we will give ourselves continually to prayer and to the ministry of the word" (Acts 6:4).

The apostles said to the Lord "Lord, teach us to pray" (Luke 11:1); and as He taught them they similarly taught others...

In the forty days after the Holy resurrection, the Lord spoke to them about everything that is related to the Kingdom of God (Acts 1:3). Prayers and the church's Sacraments must have been amongst these things. St. Paul taught the believers what is related to the Sacrament of the Eucharist, when he told them "For I received from the Lord that which I also delivered to you: that..." (1Co. 11:23).

Here, some people might ask another question; does the church exert pressure on the believer's conscience by putting forth an organized way of prayer?

Firstly, it is not about power, but guidance. Thus, the church guides her children to the appropriate way of prayer. She teaches them its aspects and spirituality, as the Lord taught His disciples the Lord's Prayer without any force on their conscience.

Secondly, every person is free to tell God whatever s/he wishes to tell in her/his own prayer; Prayers of the Hours do not stop her/him to pray her/his own prayers as well.

The church does not stop the worshipper from opening her/his heart to God, and expressing her/himself, or talking with Him about anything. In addition to that, s/he should pray the Prayers of the Hours, as it is said "These you ought to have done, without leaving the others undone" (Mat. 23:23).

So what is the wisdom of the Prayers of the Hours?

THE WISDOM OF THE PRAYERS OF THE HOURS

1. **The first wisdom is the unity of the church when praying, with one soul**

The church used to pray with "one soul" lifting up one voice to God (Acts 4:24). This will not occur unless the church is praying with one prayer, or the majority are leading the prayers and all are saying Amen. With the Agpia Prayers, the entire church prays with one heart, one mind, and one soul, lifting up to God one voice.

2. This one prayer, that is the Agpia, helps to unite the hearts in spirituality

There will be the same style in conversing with God, and in identical emotions being presented to God. The requests we ask from Him would be the same, and the spiritual lessons we learn from the Agpia will also be the same...

3. The Agpia strengthens the life of fellowship in the church

We can easily imagine thousands of worshippers together in the church all saying "Have mercy upon me O God have mercy upon me" or Kir-ye ley-son. We can also imagine millions of worshippers all around the world and its continents saying the same prayers, at the same time, and with one soul as an indication of the unity of the church and the fellowship in worship that is present in it.

4. The memory of the birth of Christ, His salvation for humanity, and His Second Coming will every day be in the minds of those worshippers who pray the Prayers of the hours

Every believer will remember the birth of Christ in the Morning Prayer, His crucifixion and death in the Prayers of the Sixth and Ninth Hours, His Second Coming in the Midnight services and many other memories.

Every believer will also remember the coming down of the Holy Spirit on the disciples at the third hour; the worshipper will then ask for the blessings and work of the Holy Spirit in her/his life. All, together, will remember the terrifying judgement day, and in fearing God will prepare for that day with repentance. All, together, will praise with the same praise as they bless the name of the Lord in the Trisagion.

5. As worshippers experience the life of fellowship when praying together, they also share the Psalms with David the prophet

They even share praises with the angels saying "Glory to God in the highest, and on earth peace, good will towards men" (Luke 2:14). All will share holy memories...and participate in the life of thanksgiving, and in waiting for the Lord...

6. We would like to say that the Agpia teaches the person to pray

It teaches the believer how to converse with God, as we will show later. It teaches the manner with which to talk with God, and offers an example of what He says and how He says it...It is in agreement with what the disciples said to the Lord "Lord, teach us how to pray".

7. The Agpia is to be taken as a way of learning, rather than a way of restriction.

It teaches the worshipper God's love, and how to desire God. It also teaches how to fear God, how to submit to Him, and how to kneel before Him. Thus, the worshipper who prays with the Agpia says: Lord, teach me Your ways, make me to understand Your ways, and guide me in an upright way...It also teaches the worshipper that God accepts sinners to Him whenever they repent, whatever or how bad her/his sin was. This is exactly the same case as with the sinful woman who washed Jesus' feet with her tears (Luke 9).

> *It teaches the worshipper God's love, and how to desire God*

8. An advantage of praying with the Agpia is that it organizes worship

Organization is very important in one's spiritual life. The Apostle warns from any person who walks without order; and he talks a lot about things that he will organize when he comes...

PRAYING ALL THE TIME

The teaching of Christ about praying all the time does not cancel the Prayers of the Hours. Practically, there is no one who prays all the time except extremely few exceptions of people who are devoted to prayer. If a person is unable to pray all the time, let her/him keep the Prayers of the Hours as a minimum. A similar example is that the commandment "Sell what you have and give to the poor" (Matt. 19:21) did not prevent one from giving the tithes and the first born, as a minimum.

Those who call for the cancellation of the Prayers of the Hours for the sake of praying all the time are only causing the majority of people to end up with nothing. This is because they cancel the Prayers of the Hours, and then cannot pray all the time. They become either confused or leave prayer to their spare times that are not organized. Meanwhile, they forget all these holy events and commemorations that are offered through the Agpia.

David the prophet was a good example of how to combine the two types of prayers. In his prayer, he says "Oh, how I love Your law" (Ps. 119); but this did not stop him from saying "Seven times a day I praise You, because of Your righteous judgements" (Ps. 119).

The Agpia Prayers are a Love Song

These Prayers are full of love that is directed towards God. It is directed towards His name, Book, commandments, house, and other holy places; it is also directed towards His angels, people, and saints.

The Agpia teaches us how to talk to God with love.

GOD'S LOVE

In our own prayers, it is very rare to talk to God about our love towards Him, but this is not the case in the Prayers of the Agpia. We say to Him "Your face, Lord, I will seek. Do not hide Your face from me; do not turn Your servant away in anger" (Ps. 27), "With my whole heart I have sought You; Oh, let me not wander from Your commandments" (Ps. 119).

Here, the worshipper does not ask for anything from God, but is asking for God Himself.

It is a high standard of prayer, getting above the level of self and worldly matters. It focuses on God Himself by asking for God; from all her/his heart, the worshipper wants the face of God because it will offer happiness.

Also the great eagerness of the worshipper towards God becomes obvious as s/he tries to be satisfied with God. The worshipper says "O God, You are my God; early will I seek You; My soul thirsts for You" "I will lift up my hands in Your name. My soul shall be satisfied as with marrow and fatness" "Therefore in the shadow of Your wings I will rejoice. My soul follows close behind You" (Ps. 63). Therefore, the worshipper calls other people to enjoy God as s/he enjoys Him "Oh, taste and see that the Lord is good" (Ps. 34).

> *The worshipper wants the face of God because it will offer happiness*

LOVING HIS WORDS AND COMMANDMENTS

Whoever loves God will also love every word that proceeds from His mouth "And in His law he meditates day and night" (Ps. 1). The worshipper loves God's commandments, rejoices in them, and finds them to be the guidance and the light that enlightens her/his way; s/he says in Psalm 19 of the Morning Prayer "The commandment of the Lord is pure, enlightening the eyes"; and "The testimony of the Lord is sure, making wise the simple; the statutes of the Lord are right, rejoicing the heart". This is why the worshipper also says in the Great Psalm and in the Midnight Prayer "Your word is a lamp to my feet and a light to my path" (Ps. 119).

Therefore, the worshipper contemplates how sweet and precious God's words are; s/he says in Psalm 19 "The judgements of the Lord are true and righteous altogether. More to be desired are they than gold, yea, than much fine gold; sweeter also than honey and the honeycomb.

The Agpia Prayers are a Love Song

Moreover by them Your servant is warned, and in keeping them there is great reward".

What the worshipper is saying, in the Great Psalm (119) about the words of God has a very deep meaning to it. In this Psalm, we say in the prayers that we lift up to God "How sweet are Your words to my taste, sweeter than honey to my mouth", "Through Your percepts I get understanding", "Remember the word to Your servant, upon which You have caused me to hope. This is comfort in my affliction, for Your word has given me life", "I am a stranger in the earth; do not hide Your commandments from me", and "I remembered Your judgements of old, O Lord, and have comforted myself". "Unless Your law had been my delight, I would then have perished in my affliction".

The worshipper talks with God about her/his love towards Him, so s/he says in Psalm 119 "Therefore, I love Your commandments more than gold, yes, than fine gold", "My soul keeps Your testimonies, and I love them exceedingly", "So shall I keep Your law continually", "And I will walk at liberty, for I seek Your precepts". "I will speak of Your testimonies also before kings, and I will not be ashamed. And I will delight myself in Your commandments, which I love. My hands also I will lift up to Your commandments, which I love, and I will meditate on Your statutes".

The worshipper contemplates on the depth and perfection of God's commandments, saying in the same Psalm "I have seen the consummation of all perfection, but Your commandment is exceedingly broad". "Open my eyes, that I may see wondrous things from Your law", "Your testimonies are wonderful; therefore my soul keeps them", "I have more understanding than all my teachers, for Your testimonies are my meditation", "I opened my mouth and panted, for I longed for Your commandments".

Praying the Agpia

What about the result of the worshipper loving God's commandments and longing for them? S/he says in the first Psalm "He shall be like a tree planted by the rivers of water, that brings forth its fruit in its season, whose leaf also shall not wither; and whatever he does shall prosper" (Ps. 1).

Because of all this, and because of our love for God's words in our prayers, we read a chapter from the Holy Gospel in every Prayer. We consider reading the Holy Gospel as part of our prayers. With time, and because of repetition, we memorize these chapters by heart, in addition to the Psalms which are also a part of the Holy Bible. By memorizing all of this, Biblical verses become part of our contemplations; with these verses we fight back any temptations that may arise against us...

As I said many times:

* Keep the Psalms protected in your hearts, and they protect you.

* Keep the Gospel protected in your hearts, and it protects you.

* The Agpia Prayers do not only train us on how to love God and His Book, but also train us on how to love His house and sanctuary.

Loving His House

There is almost no Prayer of the seven Prayers of the Agpia in which the worshipper does not mention the House of God and her/his love for it.

* In the Morning Prayer

The worshipper says "One thing I have desired of the Lord, that will I seek: that I may dwell in the house of the Lord all the days of my life, to behold the beauty of the Lord, and to inquire in His temple" (Ps. 27). Is there love for the Lord's house more than this? S/he also says "Behold, bless the Lord, all you servants of the Lord, who by night stand in the house of the Lord..." (Ps. 134, Midnight Prayer).

The worshipper also talks in Psalm 5 about entering the house of God with submission "But as for me, I will come into Your house in the multitude of Your mercy; in fear of You I will worship toward Your holy temple". Also in Psalm 15, the worshipper mentions the appropriate spiritual features that are required in whoever dwells or enters into the house of God "Lord, who may abide in Your tabernacle? Who may dwell in Your holy hill? He who walks uprightly, and works righteousness...".

There is no doubt that these are lessons we learn from the Agpia Prayers.

* In the Prayer of the Third Hour

The worshipper says "I will wash my hands in innocence; so I will go about Your altar, O Lord, that I may proclaim with the voice of thanksgiving, and tell of all Your wondrous works" (Ps. 26). S/he also says, "Lord, I have loved the habitation of Your house, and the place where Your glory dwells" (Ps. 26). "Oh, send out Your light and Your truth! Let them lead me; let them bring me to Your holy hill and to Your tabernacle. Then I will go to the altar of God, to God my exceeding joy" (Ps. 43). One other important thing about these verses, which we say in the Prayer of the Third Hour, is that we say them in the rituals of consecrating an altar.

Furthermore, in the Prayer of the Third Hour, we say "There is a river whose streams shall make glad the city of God, the holy place of the tabernacle of the Most High. God is in the midst of her, she shall not be moved" (Ps.

46). We also say "Give unto the Lord the glory due to His name; worship the Lord in the beauty of holiness" (Ps. 29). We also say in the passages of the Prayer of the Third Hour "Whenever we stand in Your Holy Temple, we are considered as those who abide in heaven".

* In the Prayer of the Sixth Hour

We say, "How lovely is Your tabernacle, O Lord of hosts! My soul longs, yes, even faints for the courts of the Lord; my heart and my flesh cry out for the living God", "Blessed are those who dwell in Your house; they will still be praising You", "For a day in Your courts is better than a thousand", and "I would rather be a doorkeeper in the house of my God than dwell in the tents of wickedness" (Ps. 84).

We also say these verses when consecrating the new altar.

In the Prayer of the Sixth Hour, we also say "His foundation is in the holy mountains. Glorious things are spoken of You, O city of God" (Ps. 87), "I will abide in Your tabernacle forever; I will trust in the shelter of Your wings" (Ps. 61). Also, "Holiness adorns Your house, O Lord, forever" (Ps. 93).

* In the Prayer of the Ninth Hour

We say "Exalt the Lord our God, and worship at His footstool; for He is holy" (Ps. 99), "Enter into His gates with thanksgiving, and into His courts with praise" (Ps. 100), and "I will offer to You the sacrifice of thanksgiving, and will call upon the name of the Lord. I will pay my vows to the Lord now in the presence of all His people, in the courts of the Lord's house, in the midst of You, O Jerusalem" (Ps. 116).

The Agpia Prayers are a Love Song

* In the Sunset Prayer

The worshipper says "Open to me the gates of righteousness; I will go through them, and I will praise the Lord. This is the gate of the Lord, through which the righteous shall enter. Blessed is he who comes in the name of the Lord! We have blessed you from the house of the Lord. Bind the sacrifice with cords to the horns of the altar" (Ps. 118).

"I was glad when they said to me: let us go into the house of the Lord" (Ps. 122).

Here, the worshipper mentions the gladness that s/he feels with the house of the Lord, and that it is a holy house, through which the righteous shall enter.

* In the Prayer of the Twelfth Hour

The worshipper says "Lord, remember David and all his afflictions; how he swore to the Lord, and vowed to the Mighty God of Jacob: Surely I will not go into the chamber of my house, or go up to the comfort of my bed; I will not give sleep to my eyes or slumber to my eyelids, until I find a place for the Lord, a dwelling place for the Mighty God of Jacob", and "Let us go into His tabernacle; let us worship at His footstool" (Ps. 132).

"Behold, how good and how pleasant it is for brethren to dwell together in unity" (Ps. 133). We also say, in Psalm 138 "Before the gods I will sing praises to You. I will worship toward Your holy temple". And in Psalm 141, the worshipper says to the Lord "Let my prayer be set before You as incense, the lifting up of my hands as the evening sacrifice". In Psalm 137, we remember that in sin we become strangers to the house of the Lord.

Praying the Agpia

Indeed, there is no way we express our love for the house of the Lord better than by the Agpia Prayers, as we pour out our emotions that are deep in our hearts.

In the Agpia there are Prayers and their Answers

These prayers contain the crying out of the worshipper, as well as the work of God for or with her/him. You find the request, as well as its rapid answer. Therefore, these prayers carry with them the spirit of hope and gladness. This is why it is very often we find the request ending with thanksgiving and joy.

The worshipper does not feel as if s/he is praying with no one to answer. To the contrary, the answer is received quickly from God. Then, the worshipper realizes that God listened to, accepted, and answered the prayer. Thus, s/he says in the Prayer of the Sixth Hour "I will hear what God the Lord will speak" (Ps. 85(84)).

The worshipper continues saying "For He will speak peace to His people and to His saints; but let them not turn back to folly" (Ps. 85(84)). It is a prayer that is combined with faith; in such a prayer, the worshipper hears - in her/his heart - what the Lord says and what He gives of peace. This is not only for the saints, but also for those who turned back to Him with repentance.

Praying the Agpia

Another good example is in the Morning Prayer, Psalm 3; the worshipper starts by mentioning her/his many tribulations saying "Lord, how they have increased who trouble me! Many are they who rise up against me. Many are they who say: there in no help for him in God". But then the worshipper says "I cried to the Lord with my voice, and He heard me from His holy hill…". S/he does not say: I cried to the Lord asking Him to answer me. Instead, s/he says, "I cried…He heard". This is wonderful; it gives the worshipper the feeling that the Agpia offers confidence in the Lord answering her/him. Thus, the worshipper says after that "The Lord sustained me. I will not be afraid of ten thousands of people who have set themselves against me all around". While the worshipper says in the beginning of the Psalm "Many are they who say: there is no help for him in God", s/he ends the Psalm with "Salvation belongs to the Lord. Your blessing is upon Your people. Alleluia".

The scenario is in Psalm 4 of the Morning Prayer as the worshipper admits that God answered her/him. S/he begins the Psalm saying "Hear me when I call, O God of my righteousness! You have delivered me when I was in distress". The worshipper also talks from experience saying "The Lord will hear me when I call to Him".

The worshipper, therefore, feels glad and grateful saying "Lord, lift up the light of Your countenance upon us. You have put gladness in my heart…I will both lie down in peace, and sleep; for You alone, O Lord, make me dwell in safety. Alleluia".

How wonderful the difference between the beginning and the end of Psalm 6 is: the Psalm is in the Morning Prayer where the worshipper says in the beginning "O Lord, do not rebuke me in Your anger, nor chasten me in Your hot displeasure. Have mercy on me, O Lord, for I am weak; O Lord, heal me, for my bones are troubled. My soul

In the Agpia there are Prayers and their Answers

also is greatly troubled; But You, O Lord-how long? Return, O Lord, deliver me". The worshipper, then, feels God's answer in the same Psalm so s/he says, "Depart from me, all you workers of iniquity; for the Lord has heard the voice of my supplication. The Lord will receive my prayer"

A worshipper may make a request in a Psalm, and find its answer in the same Psalm

(In the Arabic version, it is said "The Lord has received ..."; it is not in the future tense as in the English Agpia; Translation Note). Thus, the worshipper ends her/his prayer of the Psalm with joy, after s/he was saying "All night I make my bed swim; I drench my couch with my tears".

A worshipper may make a request in a Psalm, and find its answer in the same Psalm; but also s/he might find a second answer in another Psalm.

In the third Psalm, the worshipper says "Rise, O Lord; save me, O my God". And in Psalm 12(11), s/he hears the voice of the Lord saying "For the oppression of the poor, for the sighing of the needy, now I will arise, says the Lord, I will set him in the safety for which he yearns". This is why the worshipper rejoices in the promise of God, saying afterwards "The words of the Lord are pure words, like silver tried in a furnace of earth, purified seven times". According to God's promise, the worshipper says "You shall keep them, O Lord, You shall preserve them from this generation forever".

The same answer, and the same huge difference between the beginning and the end of the Psalm is found in Psalm 13(12), of the Morning Prayer.

The Psalm starts with great tribulations which cause the worshipper to feel as if God has forsaken her/him, so s/he says "How long, O Lord? Will You forget me forever?

How long will You hide Your face from me? How long shall I take counsel in my soul, having sorrow in my heart daily? How long will my enemy be exalted over me? Consider and hear me, O Lord my God". As soon as s/he feels that God answered her/him s/he said in the same Psalm "But I have trusted in Your mercy; my heart shall rejoice in Your salvation. I will sing to the Lord, because He has dealt bountifully with me. Alleluia".

What is this 'rejoice in salvation', and that feeling of God's blessings to the worshipper? What is this praise, singing, and rejoicing, from a person who started her/his prayer with the feeling that God has forsaken her/him, and that God has hidden His face from her/him?! It is the feeling of being listened to and being answered by God. The worshipper asks for something and is confident that God has already answered. Here, the saying of the Lord is fulfilled "Before they call, I will answer; and while they are still speaking, I will hear" (Is. 65:24).

> *The worshipper asks for something and is confident that God has already answered*

I mentioned all of this in the Morning Prayer only as examples.

The Prayer of the Third Hour starts with the Psalm of acceptance, Psalm 20(19) "May the Lord answer You in the day of trouble; may the name of the God of Jacob defend you". Then, the worshipper says "May He send you help from the sanctuary, and strengthen you out of Zion; May He remember all your offerings, and accept your burnt sacrifice. May He grant you according to your heart's desire, and fulfil all your purpose". How beautiful these words are, which are mentioned in Prayers, so that the worshipper feels God's acceptance before s/he speaks…

In the Agpia there are Prayers and their Answers

In the same Psalm, the worshipper says "Now I know that the Lord saves His anointed; He will answer him from His holy heaven with the saving strength of His right hand. These words are full of consolation and hope. The worshipper, then, says "May the King answer us when we call".

Also in Psalm 30(29) of the Prayer of the Third Hour, s/he says "O Lord my God, I cried out to You, and You have healed me. O Lord, You have brought my soul up from the grave". S/he also says "You have kept me alive, that I should not go down to the pit". When the worshipper senses any danger, s/he says "I cried out to You, O Lord; and to the Lord I made supplication: What profit is there in my blood, when I go to the pit? Will the dust praise You? Will it declare Your truth". Instantly, the worshipper feels God's answer, so s/he says "Hear, O Lord, and have mercy on me; Lord, be my helper! You have turned from me my mourning into dancing; You have put off my sackcloth and clothed me with gladness, to the end that my glory may sing praise to You and not be silent".

The worshipper announces God's answer in Psalm 34(33), and says "I sought the Lord, and He heard me, and delivered me from all my fears". S/he also says "This poor man cried out, and the Lord heard him, and saved him out of all his troubles. The angel of the Lord encamps all around those who fear Him". S/he talks about God's answer saying "The righteous cry out, and the Lord hears, and delivers them out of all their trouble. The Lord is near to those who have a broken heart, and saves such as have a contrite spirit. Many are the afflictions of the righteous, but the Lord delivers him out of them all".

The answer of the Lord is manifest in this case, even if there was no request.

We also find the answer to the prayer in the Prayer of the Sixth Hour. The first Psalm of this Prayer, Psalm 54(53), starts with the phrase "Save me, O God, by Your name... For strangers have risen up against me, and oppressors have sought after my life; they have not set God before them". Directly after this - as the worshipper knows about God's acceptance of requests, s/he says "Behold, God is my helper; the Lord is with those who uphold my life...I will praise Your name, O Lord, for it is good. For He has delivered me out of all trouble". Notice that the worshipper did not say "...will deliver...".

The following Psalm [Psalm 57(56)], in the Prayer of the Sixth Hour, shows the worshipper saying "Be merciful to me, O God, be merciful to me...". With the same feeling of God's answer, s/he says "I will cry out to God Most High, to God who performs all things for me. He shall send from heaven and save me" (In Arabic, the first phrase of the first sentence is in the present tense, while the second phrase of the first sentence as well as the second sentence are in the past tense. This indicates the continuous act of crying out to God who, we trust, has already answered the prayer. Translation Note). "God shall send forth His mercy and His truth. My soul is among lions; I lie among the sons of men who are set on fire...they have dug a pit before me; in the midst of it they themselves have fallen".

Furthermore, the worshipper says in Psalm 61(60) "Hear my cry, O God; attend to my prayer. From the end of the earth I will cry to you, when my heart is overwhelmed". Once the worshipper feels that God has answered her/him s/he says, "I will trust in the shelter of Your wings. For You, O God, have heard my vow...So I will sing praise to Your name forever, that I may daily perform my vows. Alleluia".

In the Agpia there are Prayers and their Answers

Also in Psalm 86(85) the worshipper sings of the answer of the Lord saying, "In the day of my trouble I will call upon You, for You will answer me", "Among the gods there is none like You, O Lord; nor are there any works like Your works". God Himself says in Psalm 91(90) "Because he has set his love upon Me, therefore I will deliver him; I will set him on high, because he has known My name. He shall call upon me, and I will answer him; I will be with him in trouble; I will deliver him and honor him. With long life I will satisfy him, and show him My salvation".

In the Prayer of the Ninth Hour, the worshipper realizes that answering her/his prayers led her/him to God's love, so s/he says in Psalm 116:1-9(114) "I love the Lord, because He has heard my voice and my supplications. Because He has inclined His ear to me, therefore I will call upon Him as long as I live".

In the Sunset Prayer, it is said in Psalm 120(119) "In my distress I cried to the Lord, and He heard me". In this Prayer, the worshipper talks a lot about God's blessings and feels very grateful to Him. I will talk about this point later on in the book.

The same feeling of gratitude is also obvious in the Prayer of the Twelfth Hour; the worshipper says in Psalm 138(137) "I will praise You with my whole heart...", and "Though I walk in the midst of trouble, You will revive me; You will stretch out Your hand against the wrath of my enemies, and Your right hand will save me".

Gladness and Rejoicing in the Agpia Prayers

Although the Agpia Prayers contain remorse for sins, supplication, weeping, and tears, it also contains a lot of rejoicing and gladness for the Lord and His salvation and work.

* David the prophet says in the Morning Prayer (Ps. 13(12)):

"But I have trusted in Your mercy; my heart shall rejoice in Your salvation. I will sing to the Lord, because He has dealt bountifully with me. Alleluia". In Psalm 70:4, he says "Let all those who seek You rejoice and be glad in You".

* In the Prayer on the Third Hour, the prophet says:

"Sing praise to the Lord, you saints of His, and give thanks at the remembrance of His holy name", and "You have put off my sackcloth and clothed me with gladness" (Ps. 30). He also says "Then I will go to the altar of God, to God my exceeding joy; and on the harp I will praise you, O God, my God" (Ps. 43:4).

Psalm 47, of the Prayer of the Third Hour, is full of rejoicing; David the prophet says "Oh, clap your hands, all you peoples! Shout to God with the voice of triumph...God has gone up with a shout, the Lord with the sound of a trumpet. Sing praises to God, sing praises! Sing praises to our King, sing praises! For God is the King of all the earth; sing praises with understanding".

* In the Prayer of the Sixth, he says:

"So I will sing praise to your name for ever" (Ps. 61:8). He also says "I will lift up my hands in Your name. My soul shall be satisfied as with marrow and fatness, and my mouth shall praise You with joyful lips" (Ps. 63). Furthermore, he says: "Oh, let all the nations be glad and sing for joy! For You shall judge the people righteously" (Ps. 67:4), and "Let all those who seek You rejoice and be glad in You" (Ps. 70:4).

In Psalm 86, he says "Rejoice the soul of Your servant, for to You, O Lord, I lift up my soul", and "Unite my heart to fear Your name". In this Sixth Hour, the time when the Lord was crucified, the prophet rejoices with his salvation which is also for all peoples. He also rejoices with the help and protection of the Lord, as in Psalm 91.

* The Prayer of the Ninth Hour is full of praises and gladness.

The prophet says "The Lord reigns; let the earth rejoice; let the multitude of isles be glad... Light is sown for the righteous, and gladness for the upright in heart. Rejoice in the Lord, you righteous, and give thanks at the remembrance of his holy name" (Ps. 97). He also says "Zion hears and is glad, and the daughters of Judah rejoice" (Ps. 97).

Gladness and Rejoicing in the Agpia Prayers

It is the time when the Lord paid the price of our sins, by His death on the cross for our sake.

This is why David the prophet says in Psalm 98 "All the ends of the earth have seen the salvation of our God. Shout joyfully to the Lord, all the earth; break forth in song, rejoice, and sing praises. Sing to the Lord with the harp, with the harp and the sound of a psalm, with trumpets and the sound of a horn; Shout joyfully before the Lord, the King... Let the rivers clap their hands; let the hills be joyful together before the Lord". Furthermore, the prophet says in Psalm 100 "Make a joyful shout to the Lord, all you lands! Serve the Lord with gladness; come before His presence with singing". The rest of the Psalms in the Prayer of the Ninth Hour also talk about the salvation of the Lord.

* Also in the Sunset Prayer

We say "This is the day which the Lord has made; we will rejoice and be glad in it" (Ps. 118:24). We also say "I was glad when they said to me: let us go into the house of the Lord" (Ps. 122:1). David the prophet mentions the remembrance of the Lord's blessings and His help a lot of times; he says: "When the Lord brought back the captivity of Zion, we were like those who dream. Then our mouth was filled with laughter, and our tongue with singing. Then they said among the nations: the Lord has done great things for them. The Lord has done great things for us, whereof we are glad...Those who sow in tears shall reap in joy" (Ps. 126).

It is good to end the day praying with the Agpia with Joy. We remember the blessings of God because "If it had not been the Lord who was on our side when men rose up against us, then they would have swallowed us alive...The snare is broken, and we have escaped" (Ps. 124).

* The Prayer of the Twelfth Hour too has a lot of praises, confession to the Lord and remembering His abundant blessings.

Many of the Psalms in this Prayer start with praises such as "Praise the Lord! Praise the Lord, O my soul", "Praise the Lord! For it is good to sing praises to our God", and "Praise the Lord, O Jerusalem! Praise your God, O Zion"...

Talking about God's blessings is also frequent in this Prayer. Examples include; "Who executes justice for the oppressed...The Lord gives freedom to the prisoners... The Lord raises those who are bowed down...The Lord watches over the strangers; He relieves the fatherless and widow" (Ps. 146(145)), and "He strengthened the bars of your gates; He blessed your children within you. He makes peace in your borders, and fills you with the finest wheat" (Ps. 147).

Praise is also frequent in the Midnight Prayer. An example is the Great Psalm (119); it is full of praise.

In the Agpia Prayers, we get Reassurance about God's Promises, so we Become Glad

There is no doubt that the promises of God fill the soul with reassurance, because they are true. The Agpia Prayers are full of these promises which when remembered by the worshipper, her/his heart becomes filled with hope and gladness. St. Paul the apostle said "Rejoice in hope" (Rom. 12:12).

What are these promises then, that reassure the worshipper in her/his prayers in the Agpia?

God's Promises

In the Morning Prayer, the second Psalm, the worshipper listens to the Godly saying, "The Lord has said to me, you are My son, today I have begotten you. Ask of me and I give you the nations of your inheritance...". Although the verse is a prophecy about Jesus Christ, it also gives the worshipper hope. Similarly, the prophet's saying about His enemies "He who sits in the heavens shall laugh; the Lord shall hold them in derision. Then, He shall speak to them in His wrath, and distress them in His deep displeasure".

In Psalm 12(11), the prophet listens to the Godly voice saying "For the oppression of the poor, for the sighing of the needy, now I will arise, says the Lord; I will set him in the safety for which he yearns". This is a verse full of consolation that fills the heart with hope in the Lord's salvation, whatever the surrounding adversities may be.

In the Prayer of the Third Hour, there are a lot of Psalms that are full of Godly promises. All of them are full of encouragement, hope, help, and answers for the requests. One of these Psalms is Psalm 20(19), where the Godly voice says;

* "May the Lord answer you in the day of trouble; may the name of the God of Jacob defend".

* "May He send you help from the sanctuary, and strengthen you out of Zion".

* "May He remember all your offerings and accept your burnt sacrifice".

* "May He grant you according to your heart's desires, and fulfil all your purpose".

* "May the Lord fulfil all your petitions"...until He says "Now I know that the Lord saves His anointed; He will answer him from His holy heaven with the saving strength of His right hand".

* "Some trust in chariots, and some in horses; but we will remember the name of the Lord our God".

* "They have bowed down and fallen; but we have risen and stand upright".

Reassurance about God's Promises

I advise every worshipper to say this Psalm during her/his troubles and adversities. I also advise every priest to say it on the heads of his children during their troubles and adversities.

In the Prayer of the Third Hour, we find that Psalm 34(33) is full of God's promises and encouragement; the worshipper will find in it what s/he needs to be reassured;

* "The angel of the Lord encamps all around those who fear Him, and delivers them".

* "There is no want in those who fear Him".

* "Those who seek the Lord shall not lack any good thing".

* "The eyes of the Lord are on the righteous, and His ears are open to their cry".

* "The Lord is near to those who have a broken heart, and saves such as have a contrite spirit".

* "Many are the afflictions of the righteous, but the Lord delivers him out of them all".

* "He guards all his bones; not one of them is broken".

* "The Lord redeems the soul of His servants, and none of those who trust in Him shall be condemned".

For all of those beautiful and many promises, we see that the worshipper starts her/his prayer in this Psalm with the verse "I will bless the Lord at all times; His praise shall continually be in my mouth. My soul shall make its boast in the Lord".

Also in the Third Hour, the worshipper feels as if the promises of God are a window in her/his life, so s/he says in Psalm 23(22) "The Lord is my shepherd; I shall not want". The worshipper, then, elaborates on that saying "He makes me to lie down in green pastures; He leads me beside the still waters. He restores my soul; He leads me in the paths of righteousness for His name's sake".

Her/his reassurance builds up until it reaches a climax when s/he says to the Lord "Yea, though I walk through the valley of the shadow of death, I will fear no evil; for You are with me; Your rod and Your staff, they comfort me". And also "Mercy shall follow me all the days of my life". The worshipper, here, is not only mentioning the promises of God, but also testing how effective they are in her/his life.

The same thing occurs in praying with Psalm 29(28), when the worshipper says "The voice of the Lord is powerful; the voice of the Lord is full of majesty", and "The voice of the Lord divides the flames of fire. The voice of the Lord shakes the wilderness". The fathers used this verse every time they felt any danger surrounding them. They felt that a Godly power was around them.

Furthermore, in Psalm 46(45) of the Prayer of the Third Hour, the worshipper feels God's help that He promised, so the worshipper becomes reassured and says, "God is my refuge and strength, a very present help in trouble. Therefore we will not fear, though the earth is removed, and though the mountains be carried into the midst of the sea". Also, s/he says "The Lord of hosts is with us; The God of Jacob is our refuge", and "There is a river whose streams shall make glad the city of God, the holy place of the tabernacle of the Most High. God is in the midst of her, she shall not be moved; God shall help her, just at the break of dawn".

These are the promises that give the worshipper reassurance and hope...

Reassurance about God's Promises

Also in the Gospel of the Prayer of the Third Hour, the worshiper finds Godly promises about the work of the Holy Spirit in, and for, us; s/he also finds other promises from the Lord Jesus.

The worshipper says "He will teach you all things, and bring to your remembrance all things that I said to you". Also s/he listens to other promises from the Lord "Peace I leave with you, My peace I give to you", and "Let not your heart be troubled, neither let it be afraid" (John 14).

Furthermore, we hear other Godly promises in the Prayer of the Sixth Hour. The worshipper says in Psalm 85(84) "I will hear what God the Lord will speak, for He will speak peace to His people and His saints; but let them not turn back to folly. Surely His salvation is near those who fear Him, that glory may dwell in our land".

Also in Psalm 91(90), there are a lot of divine promises that divine revelation speaks of to the worshipper "He shall cover you with His feathers, and under His wings you shall take refuge", and "His truth shall be your shield and buckler. You shall not be afraid of the terror by night, nor of the arrow that flies by day, nor the pestilence that walks in darkness, nor of the destruction that lays waste at noonday". Moreover, the worshipper says "A thousand may fall at your side, and ten thousand at your right hand; but it shall not come near you. Only with your eyes shall you look, and see the reward of the wicked", and "No evil shall befall you, nor shall any plague come near your dwelling".

Furthermore, s/he says "For He shall give His angels charge over you, to keep you in all your ways. They shall bear you up in their hands, lest you dash your foot against a stone", "You shall tread upon the lion and the cobra, the young lion and the serpent you shall trample underfoot",

"Because he has set his love upon Me, therefore I will deliver him; I will set him on high because he has known My name", and "He shall call upon Me, and I will answer him; I will be with him in trouble; I will deliver him and honor him. With long life I will satisfy him, and show him My salvation, Alleluia".

If the person improvised her/his prayer, that is, prayed without the Psalms of the Agpia, do you think s/he would have enjoyed hearing all these promises, become reassured and rejoiced? We also should not forget the Beatitudes that are in the Gospel of the Sixth Hour (Mat. 5:3-12), and what they offer of God's promises.

In the Prayer of the Ninth Hour, in Psalm 97(96), the Divine inspiration says "He preserves the souls of His saints; He delivers them out of the hand of the wicked. Light is sown for the righteous, and gladness for the upright in heart". God repeats this promise in Psalm 112(111) of the Prayer of the Ninth Hour. Also in Psalm 113(112), God gives hope to those who are humble as He says "Who is like the Lord our God, who dwells on high, who humbles himself to behold the things that are in the heavens and in the earth", and "He raises the poor out of the dust, and lifts the needy out of the rubbish heap, that He may seat him with princes - with the princes of His people. He grants the barren woman a home, like a joyful mother of children". In Psalm 116:1-9(114), God says: "He will bless those who fear the Lord, both small and great".

In the Sunset Prayer, the promises that are in Psalm 121(120) are very beautiful and many; God says "He will not allow your foot to be moved; He who keeps you will not slumber".

Reassurance about God's Promises

* "The Lord is your keeper; the Lord is your shade at your right hand. The sun shall not strike you by day, nor the moon by night".

* "The Lord shall preserve you from all evil; He shall preserve your soul".

* "The Lord shall preserve your going out and your coming in from this time forth, and even forever more. Alleluia".

I also hope that all priests memorize this Psalm, to pray with it on the heads of anyone who asks them to pray for her/him.

In Psalm 125(124), the worshipper says "Those who trust in the Lord are like Mount Zion, which cannot be moved, but abides forever", and "The scepter of wickedness shall not rest on the land allotted to the righteous". In Psalm 126(125), s/he says, "Those who sow in tears shall reap in joy". Also in Psalm 128(127), there are a lot of God's promises;

* "When you eat the labor of your hands, you shall be happy, and it shall be well with you".

* "Your wife shall be like a fruitful vine in the very heart of your house".

* "Your children like olive plants all around your table".

* "Behold, thus shall the man be blessed who fears the Lord".

In the Prayer of the Twelfth Hour, the worshipper sings with the promises of the Lord or His blessings. S/he says in Psalm 146(145) "Who keeps truth for ever, who executes justice for the oppressed", "Who gives food for the hungry. The Lord gives freedom to the prisoners... The

Praying the Agpia

Lord raises those who are bowed down", and "The Lord watches over the strangers; He relieves the fatherless and widow".

Furthermore, there are a lot of similar promises in Psalm 147:1-11(146); "He heals the broken hearted, and binds up their wounds", and "The Lord lifts up the humble; He casts the wicked down to the ground". God is also the one "Who makes grass to grow on the mountains"; "He gives to the beast its food, and to the young ravens that cry".

If God does all of this to the beasts and ravens, wouldn't He do more for the human being whom He created in His own image?!

How beautiful it is to listen to the promises of the Lord during our prayer with the Agpia

In Psalm 147:12-20, God says about Jerusalem and Zion, the symbols of the Church and the human soul "Praise the Lord, O Jerusalem! Praise your God, O Zion", and "For He has strengthened the bars of your gates; He has blessed your children within you". This means that the Lord is the one who shuts the gates of the mind and the heart before all sinful desires; He is the one to bless your children, that is your virtues that are born of the Holy Spirit within you.

There are also a lot of promises that the worshipper with the Agpia finds in the Midnight Prayer. These include promises for the remission of sins, such as the case with the sinful woman who washed the Lord's feet with her tears; He told her "your sins are forgiven" (Luke 7). Another example is when the Lord said to Simon the Pharisee regarding the two debtors "And when they had nothing with which to repay, he freely forgave them both" (Luke 7). Also the Lord's promises when He says in Luke 12 "Do not fear, little flock, for it is your Father's good pleasure to give you the kingdom". Furthermore, He says, "Blessed

Reassurance about God's Promises

are those servants whom the master, when he comes, will find watching"; also His beatitude for "the wise steward, whom his master will make ruler over his household, to give them their food in due season".

This is why we mention, in the absolution of the Midnight Prayer, what the Lord says in His Second Coming "Come you that are blessed by my Father! Come and inherit the Kingdom that has been prepared for you since the creation of the world".

How beautiful it is to listen to the promises of the Lord during our prayer with the Agpia. These promises make us attached to God through love; they give us reassurance and hope. Also, they make us thankful and grateful to the Lord.

The promises of God in the Agpia are not theoretical, but rather are mingled with our long experience in God's answers to us. We explained this in a previous chapter.

The promises of God strengthen us and allow us to rely on Him in our everyday lives. This reliance on God is the topic of our next chapter of our contemplations on the Agpia.

In the Agpia, there is Complete Reliance on God

There is an inclusive and determining statement that invites us to completely rely on God; it is in Psalm 127(126) in the Sunset Prayer. The worshipper says, "Unless the Lord builds the house, they labor in vain who build it; unless the Lord guards the city, the watchman stays awake in vain".

The entire Agpia contains statements that invite us to rely on God.

In the Morning Prayer, we say in Psalm 25(24) "Let me not be ashamed, for I put my trust in You". Also in the same Psalm "O my God, I trust in You; let me not be ashamed; let not my enemies triumph over me. Indeed, let no one who waits on You be ashamed".

We find that reliance on God, in this Psalm, is mingled with hope and trust in the works of God. Therefore, s/he will not be ashamed as long as s/he is relying on God; that is, s/he will not be let down due to her/his reliance on the Lord or waiting for Him.

Praying the Agpia

In one of the Psalms, Psalm 26(25), of the Prayer of the Third Hour, the worshipper says: "Vindicate me, O Lord, for I have walked in my integrity. I have also trusted in the Lord". The worshipper not only invites her/himself to rely on God, but also invites others and blesses them for relying on God. S/he says in Psalm 34(33) "Oh, taste and see that the Lord is good", and "Blessed is the man who trusts in the Lord".

In the Prayer of the Sixth Hour, the worshipper says in Psalm 57(56) "Be merciful to me, O God, be merciful to me! For my soul trusts in You; and in the shadow of Your wings I will make my refuge, until these calamities have passed by". The worshipper considers reliance on God as a justifying reason for God's mercy.

This might be similar to what we pray in the Midnight Prayer (Ps. 119) "Remember the word to Your servant, upon which You have caused me to hope", and "This is my comfort in my affliction, for Your word has given me life". Also in the same Psalm (Ps. 119:41,42) "Let Your mercies come also to me, O Lord-Your salvation according to Your word. So shall I also have an answer for him who reproaches me, for I trust in Your word".

Furthermore, still in the Prayer of the Sixth Hour, the worshipper says in Psalm 86(85) "Save Your servant who trusts in You". This is because salvation is from the Lord. S/he also says in Psalm 118(117) of the Sunset Prayer "The Lord is my strength and song, and He has become my salvation"

In Psalm 91(90) of the Prayer of the Sixth Hour, the worshipper says "I will say of the Lord: He is my refuge and my fortress; my God, in Him I will trust. Surely He shall deliver you from the snare of the fowler. And from the perilous pestilence".

Complete Reliance on God

It is commonsense that if we consider God to be our refuge and fortress that we would trust in Him, especially if we have some temptations in our spiritual lives; He will save us from the snare of the fowler.

There are some experiences, in the Sunset Prayer, about the fact that reliance on God is better than relying on humans, and that those who rely on God are strong.

In regard to this point, the worshipper says in Psalm 118(117) "It is better to trust in the Lord than to put confidence in man. It is better to trust in the Lord than to put confidence in princes". S/he also says in the same Prayer, in Psalm 125(124) "Those who trust in the Lord are like Mount Zion, which cannot be moved, but abides forever".

Moreover, s/he says in Psalm 146(145) of the Prayer of the Twelfth Hour "Do not put your trust in princes, nor in a son of man, in whom there is no help. His spirit departs, he returns to his earth; in that very day his plans perish". The worshipper, then, says "Happy is he who has the God of Jacob for his help, who made heaven and earth, the sea, and all that is in them". These statements about the might of the Creator confirm our need to rely on Him.

This is why during tribulations the worshipper relies on the Lord; s/he says in Psalm 141(140) of the Prayer of the Twelfth Hour "But my eyes are upon You, O God the Lord; in You I take refuge...Keep me from the snares which they have laid for me, and from the traps of the workers of iniquity".

The worshipper continues in Psalm 142(141) saying "In the way in which I walk they have secretly set a snare for me. Look on my right hand and see, for there is no one who acknowledges me; refuge has failed me; no one cares for my soul. I cried out to You, O Lord; I said 'You are my refuge, my portion in the land of the living'". Furthermore,

Praying the Agpia

in the passage "Lord, by Your grace..." at the end of the Prayer of the Twelfth Hour the worshipper says "Lord, let Your mercy on us be as great as our reliance on You". S/he also says, "Save me Lord, for I am seeking You".

The Agpia is a School of Faith

The church teaches us, through the Agpia Prayers, that our prayers cannot be separate from our Faith and that dogmatic faith is part of prayer. We believe in God, so we converse with Him in our prayers. This God, in whom we believe, is talked about in detail in the Agpia Prayers.

Therefore, the Agpia is a lesson in Faith; the more we pray from the Agpia, the deeper we become in the Faith. Indeed, we understand the Faith through the rituals of the church as well as through the Bible, dogmatic books, and the teachings of the Fathers.

What principles of Faith does the Agpia offer to us?

The Creed

In the Agpia, we recite the Creed as part of our prayers.

By doing this, we remember who this God is whom we pray to. We also proclaim this every time we pray as a congregation. Thus, our prayers would be derived from a correct Faith...if a heresy or a blasphemy appears against that Faith, we would be protected from it through those Prayers in the Agpia.

Reciting the Creed is not only in the Prayers of the Hours, but also in all Holy Masses, in every Sacrament of the Church, in all liturgies, and in all our spiritual meetings.

In the Creed, we remember that we worship one God; we also remember the Holy Trinity: the Father, the Son, and the Holy Spirit. We also remember the Incarnation, Crucifixion, Redemption, Resurrection, Salvation, Baptism, Second Coming, Resurrection of the Dead, life of the world to come...etc. All of these facts of the Faith become well established in our minds every day and every hour...

The Dogma of the Holy Trinity

We remember this dogma and recite it several times in the Prayers of the Hours (the Agpia).

We start our Prayer with the statement "In the name of the Father, and the Son, and the Holy Spirit, One God, Amen".

In the Trisagion, we pray to the Holy Trinity saying "O' Holy Trinity, have mercy on us".

We conclude the Thanksgiving Prayer by saying "Glory, honor, dominion and worship are due to You together with Him and the Life Giving and consubstantial Holy Spirit...". Furthermore, in the passage of "Lord, by Your grace..." at the end of the Prayer of the Twelfth Hour, we say "Blessing, praise and glory are due to You, O' Father and Son and the Holy Spirit who is being since the beginning, now, and forever. Amen".

In the Absolution of the Sunset Prayer, we pray to the Son saying "At all times and everywhere we glorify and praise

The Agpia is a School of Faith

Your name, Your Father and the Holy Spirit forevermore. Amen". Moreover, we pray to the Son, in the Absolution of the Prayer of the Veil, saying "Grant us glorification in the whole night to bless Your Holy Name, full of glory and majesty with Your Gracious Father and the Holy Spirit now and forever more. Amen". Also, in the Introduction of the Midnight Prayer, we say "Glory be to the Father and to the Son and to the Holy Spirit, now and forever more…Glory be to the Holy Trinity, have mercy upon us".

We pray to the Holy Trinity, glorify the Holy Trinity, and start our prayers in the Name of the Holy Trinity. We do this by saying "O' Holy Trinity" or "In the Name of the Father and the Son and the Holy Spirit".

As we pray to the Holy Trinity, we also pray to each Hypostasis individually. We say to the Father in the Absolution of the Prayer of the Sixth Hour "We give thanks to You Our Almighty King, Father of our Lord and Savior Jesus Christ, and we glorify You for You have made the hours of suffering of Your Only Begotten Son a time of prayer and comfort".

We pray to Him in the Absolution of the Prayer of the Ninth Hour saying "O' God, the Father of our Lord, God and Savior Jesus Christ…Receive our prayers at all times and this prayer of the ninth hour".

The Thanksgiving Prayer that we say in the introduction of each Prayer of the Hours is also directed to God the Father. We say "Let us give thanks to the gracious and merciful God, the Father of our Lord, God and Savior Jesus Christ…". We also say "O Lord, Master and Almighty God, the Father of our Lord, God and Savior Jesus Christ, we thank You…". There are many prayers that are directed to God the Father.

Praying the Agpia

The prayers that are directed to the Son are also many. We say to Him in the passages of the Morning Prayer "O true light that enlightens every man that comes into the world. You came to the world because of Your love to mankind, and all the creation rejoiced at Your coming...". We also say "When the morning hour approaches, O' Christ our God the True Light, let the senses and the thoughts of the light shine upon us...".

Furthermore, we say at the conclusion of every Prayer "Have mercy upon us O' God, have mercy upon us. For You are always worshipped and glorified in heaven and on earth. O' Christ, our good Lord, plenteous in patience, mercy and compassion...".

We also say the passages of the Prayer of the Sixth Hour to the Son. For example, we say "Lord, who on the sixth day, at the sixth hour You were nailed to the Cross for the sin that Adam dared to commit in paradise...". We also say "O' Lord Christ, You gave salvation to the whole world when You spread Your undefiled hands on the cross... we worship Your incorruptible person, praying for the remission of our sins...".

Passages of the Prayer of the Ninth Hour are also directed to the Son; we say "O' Lord who tasted death in the flesh at the ninth hour for our sake, we the sinners; mortify our carnal senses...". We also say "You surrendered Your soul to the hands of the father, after being hung on the cross...", "You were born of the virgin, for our sake and endured crucifixion, O' righteous Lord...Do not turn Your face from those whom You made by Your hands...", and "O' righteous Lord who received the confession of the thief on the cross, accept us...".

In the passages of the Sunset Prayer, we say "Take me now, my Savior into Your Fatherly embrace...".

The Agpia is a School of Faith

The same thing occurs in the rest of the Prayers, as previously mentioned.

Directing prayers to the Holy Spirit is very obvious in the Prayer of the Third Hour; "O' heavenly King, the comforter, the Spirit of truth, who is everywhere and fills everybody. You are the treasure of goodness and giver of life, we ask You to graciously come and dwell within us, purify us from iniquity and save our souls". This passage is repeated in the three services of the Midnight Prayer. We also mention the grace of the Holy Spirit in the conclusion of the Prayer of the Third Hour.

Directing our prayers to each Hypostasis of the Holy Trinity is a teaching that the Agpia offers to us. We also learn this from the Holy mass and many ritual prayers.

The Agpia also shows us a lot of the Divine characteristics, some of which we mentioned previously. These characteristics are in the passages of the Prayers, the Trisagion, or at the conclusion of each Prayer. We say of the Lord Christ that He is the Holy Almighty who is the Holy Immortal. We also mention that He is eternal, as we remember His Divinity, Incarnation, and His Creation of the world (in the Gospel of the Morning Prayer). Moreover, we say that He is the True Light, the Savior who carried the sins of the world, the Word (Logos); we also mention His priesthood "You are a priest forever according to the order of Melchizedek" (Ps. 110). Furthermore, we mention His Second Coming in the Midnight Prayer, as we mention His relationship to mankind at the conclusion of each Prayer.

We mention a lot of dogmas about the Lord Christ when reciting the Creed. We say of the Father that He is the Lord of Hosts, existing before all ages and forever, the Pantocrator who sends light to all of us. We mention the characteristics of the Holy Spirit in the Prayer of the Third Hour.

Indeed, we learn theology from praying with the Agpia.

We learn something about God's attitude towards mankind, and that He is "who does not wish death for the sinner but repentance and life, calling us all to salvation for the promised forthcoming rewards". We also recognize the correct faith through Him; His Holy Spirit teaches us to "worship the Holy Trinity in one divinity and one nature". We say "One Lord, one faith, one baptism" (Eph. 4:5).

Theological education in the Prayers of the Hours is not restricted to the Holy Trinity, but also dwells in teachings about St. Mary and the saintly angels.

St. Mary and the Angels

We mention St. Mary in the third passage of each Prayer, asking for her intercession.

We mention that she is the ever-virgin Mother, the pure saint, and Mother of God the intercessor. We also say that she is the honorable Mother of the light; and that everywhere under the sun people offer her glorification; she is the second heaven, full of grace, and the true vine that carries the fruit of life. We acknowledge that the Father chose her, the Holy Spirit over shadowed her and the Son, in humility, was incarnated from her. Furthermore, we mention that she is the gate of heaven; her supplications are many and are acceptable to our Savior; she is a capable, merciful and helpful Mother; and that she is the bastion of our salvation, our impregnable fortress, Mother of mercy and salvation, and gate of life.

We also mention the saintly angels in the Agpia.

The Agpia is a School of Faith

We sing praises together with them saying "Let us sing with the angels..."; we ask God saying "surround us with Your holy angels that we may be guided and guarded with them...".

Furthermore, we mention what was said about them, and about them protecting us, in the Psalms of David.

In the Agpia, there is Thanksgiving and Gratitude

Many people ask for different things in their prayers, yet rarely thank! On the other hand, the worshipper who uses the Agpia mentions God's gifts to her/him; hence, starts to thank Him for all that He has done. S/he will feel grateful, rejoicing and praising.

Very often, rejoicing and praise accompany our thanksgiving.

The worshipper even starts with the Prayer of Thanksgiving, which includes a lot of details. The worshipper thanks God "On every occasion, in every condition and for all things". Here, we feel that the worshipper is grateful, regardless of the state that s/he is in. S/he does not protest, but rather accepts everything that God offers her/him, with thanksgiving.

The worshipper elaborates on the reasons behind her/his thanksgiving; s/he says to the Lord "For You have protected, assisted, preserved, accepted us, had compassion upon us and brought us till this hour". I refer the reader to our book Prayer of Thanksgiving for contemplations on these words.

* Prayer of Thanksgiving is not the end of the matter; but in every Prayer of the Agpia there will be thanksgiving, be it in Psalms, Absolutions, or the Passages.

* In the Absolution of the Morning Prayer, the worshipper says "We thank You our eternal King, for You passed us through the night in peace and brought us to the beginning of this day".

* In the Absolution of the Prayer of the Third Hour, s/he says "We give You thanks for raising us up for prayer at this holy hour. At this hour You poured the rich grace of Your Holy Spirit in the shape of tongues of fire on Your saintly disciples and honorable apostles".

* In the Absolution of the Prayer of the Sixth Hour, the worshipper says "We give thanks to You our Almighty King...and we glorify You for You have made the hours of suffering of Your Only Begotten Son a time of prayer and comfort".

* In the Absolution of the Sunset Prayer, the worshipper says "Thank You, compassionate Lord, for You granted us to pass this day in peace, brought us thankfully to the night and made us worthy of seeing Your light until sunset".

* In the Passage "Lord, by Your grace...", at the end of the Prayer of the Twelfth Hour, s/he says "It is good to confess to the Lord and to praise Your name, O Most High, Your mercy is declared in the mornings and Your justice every night".

* In the Psalms of every Hour, the worshipper shows that s/he is grateful to God;

Thanksgiving and Gratitude

THE MORNING PRAYER

The worshipper says in Psalm 16(15) "I will bless the Lord who has given me counsel". Also, s/he says, "I set the Lord always before me; because He is at my right hand I shall not be moved. Therefore my heart is glad, and my glory rejoices...You will show me the path of life; my flesh also will rest in hope". Here, the worshipper admits that God has helped her/him and granted her/him understanding, protection, and showed her/him the path of life. The worshipper mixes her/his thanksgiving with gladness and rejoicing.

THE PRAYER OF THE THIRD HOUR

In Psalm 23(22), the worshipper mentions God's help and gifts saying "The Lord is my shepherd; I shall not want. He makes me to lie down in green pastures; He leads me besides the still waters. He restores my soul; He leads me in the paths of righteousness...". The worshipper admits the perfection of God's caring that made her/him not in need of anything, for God grants her/him the spiritual food, protects, and guides her/him so that the worshipper does not go astray.

In Psalm 30(29), the worshipper says "I will extol You, O Lord, for You have lifted me up, and have not let my foes rejoice over me...O Lord, You have brought my soul up from the grave; You have kept me alive, that I should not go down to the pit...Lord, be my helper! You have turned for me my mourning into dancing". The worshipper mentions that God granted her/him salvation, help, and rejoicing; hence, s/he says "To the end that my glory may sing praise to You and not be silent. O Lord my God, I will give thanks to You". We see that the worshipper mixed praising God with acknowledging His salvation, and rejoicing.

In Psalm 29(28), the worshipper does not only thank God for His works with her/him alone, but also thanks Him for the works done for the whole Church, the congregation. S/he says "The Lord will give strength to His people; the Lord will bless His people with peace".

THE PRAYER OF THE SIX HOUR

The worshipper says in Psalm 54(53) "Behold, God is my helper; the Lord is with those who uphold my life. He will repay my enemies for their evil...I will praise Your name, O Lord...For He has delivered me out of all trouble; and my eye has seen its desire upon my enemies".

Also, in Psalm 57(56), the worshipper says "I will cry out to God Most High, to God who performs all things for me; He reproaches the one who would swallow me up. God shall send forth His mercy and His truth. My soul is among lions; I lie among the sons of men who are set on fire".

Here, the worshipper mentions how God has delivered her/him from tribulations and from all enemies. S/he mentions that her/his deliverance was sent from heaven.

The worshipper does not forget God's help, so s/he will always be grateful to Him. In Psalm 61(60), s/he asks God to "Lead me to the rock that is higher than I. For You have been a shelter for me, and a strong tower from the enemy". Consequently, the worshipper says, "So I will sing praises to Your name forever, that I may daily perform my vows".

In the passages of the Prayer of the Sixth Hour, the worshipper thanks God when s/he remembers God's redemption that was offered on the cross; s/he says "... You were pleased to willingly go to the cross to rescue Your creation from the slavery of the enemy. We thank

Thanksgiving and Gratitude

You Christ, for You filled us all with joy, when You came to help the world, Glory be to You".

PRAYER OF THE NINTH HOUR

The worshipper praises the works that the Lord is doing for her/him; s/he says in Psalm 116:1-9(114) "I love the Lord, because He has heard my voices and my supplications. Because He has inclined His ear to me, therefore I will call upon Him as long as I live". Then, s/he explains how the Lord has saved her/him; s/he says "The pains of death encompassed me, and the pangs of Sheol laid hold of me; I found trouble and sorrow. Then I called upon the name of the Lord: O Lord, I implore You, deliver my soul", and "Gracious is the Lord, and righteous; yes, our God is merciful". The worshipper keeps explaining until s/he says, "For the Lord has dealt bountifully with you. For You have delivered my soul from death, my eyes from tears, and my feet from falling. I will walk before the Lord in the land of the living. Alleluia".

This Psalm is about the Lord delivering from death, and from Hades.

Following this Psalm is Psalm 116:10-19(115), in which the worshipper says, "What shall I render to the Lord for all His benefits toward me? I will take up the cup of salvation, and call upon the name of the Lord. I will pay my vows to the Lord now in the presence of all His people". Then, with gratitude, s/he says, "You have loosed my bonds. I will offer to You the sacrifice of thanksgiving, and will call upon the name of the Lord. I will pay my vows to the Lord now in the presence of all His people, in the courts of the Lord's house".

Feeling grateful, in this case, is expressed in the form of praises, paying the vows, and calling upon the name of the Lord; all of this is done in the presence of all His people.

Praying the Agpia

THE SUNSET PRAYER

This Prayer contains a lot of details about gratitude.

The worshipper mentions God's blessings to her/him, and that without God s/he would not have been saved from the enemies that are stronger and mightier than her/him. The worshipper says in Psalm 118(117) "The right hand of the Lord does valiantly. The right hand of the Lord is exalted; the right hand of the Lord does valiantly. I shall not die, but live, and declare the works of the Lord", and "You pushed me violently, that I might fall, but the Lord helped me".

The worshipper explains how her/his enemies fought with her/him violently, and how the Lord delivered her/him from them. After this explanation, the worshipper praises, rejoices, and acknowledges gratefully the works of the Lord.

The worshipper says "They surrounded me, yes, they surrounded me; but in the name of the Lord I will destroy them. They surrounded me like bees; they were quenched like a fire of thorns; for in the name of the Lord I will destroy them". Their fights with the worshipper end when s/he says "The Lord is my strength and song, and He has become my salvation. The voice of rejoicing and salvation is in the tents of the righteous", "I will praise You, for You have answered me, and have become my salvation", "You are my God, and I will praise You; You are my God, I will exalt You", and "This is the day which the Lord has made; we will rejoice and be glad in it". The worshipper invites all people to join her/him in this thanksgiving; s/he says, "Oh, give thanks to the Lord, for He is good! For His mercy endures forever". This invitation is made at the beginning of the Psalm as it is made at its end.

Thanksgiving and Gratitude

Indeed, acknowledging God and feeling grateful to Him is extensive in the Psalms of the Sunset Prayer. One of the most obvious statements of gratitude is what the worshipper says in Psalm 124(123) "If it had not been the Lord who was on our side, when men rose up against us, they would have swallowed us alive, when their wrath was kindled against us". S/he also says "Blessed be the Lord, who has not given us as prey to their teeth", "Our soul has escaped as a bird from the snare of the fowlers", and "The snare is broken, and we have escaped. Our help is in the name of the Lord, who made heaven and earth. Alleluia".

The worshipper, indeed, sings joyfully of the power of God that works with her/his human weakness. S/he sings of the salvation that God offered to her/him when s/he was greatly lost. God did not give her/him as prey to the teeth of her/his enemies...

The worshipper also sings of this in Psalm 126(125) saying "The Lord has done great things for us, whereof we are glad". Furthermore, s/he mentions God's help in Psalm 129(128) saying "Many a time they have afflicted me from my youth...

> *The worshipper, indeed, sings joyfully of the power of God that works with her/his human weakness*

Many a time they have afflicted me from my youth; yet they have not prevailed against me. The plowers plowed on my back; they made their furrows long. The Lord is righteous; He has cut in pieces the cords of the wicked". Those "wicked" might have been the devils that attack her/his soul. The wicked might also be the sinful desires and ideas that the worshipper is trying to keep away.

Praying the Agpia

THE PRAYER OF THE TWELFTH HOUR

Gratitude is obvious in many Psalms. For example, the worshipper says in Psalm 138(137) "I will praise You with my whole heart; before the gods I will sing praises to You...and praise Your name for Your loving kindness and Your truth". S/he also says "Though I walk in the midst of trouble, You will revive me; You will stretch out Your hand against the wrath of my enemies, and Your right hand will save me".

Psalm 146(145) is full of praises; the worshipper says, "Praise the Lord! Praise the Lord, O my soul! While I live I will praise the Lord...". Why?

"For He has strengthened the bars of your gates; He has blessed Your children within you", and "He makes peace in your borders, and fills you with the finest wheat" (Ps. 147:12-20).

Praises in the Agpia

The Midnight Prayer, the Morning Prayer, Prayers of the day (Third, Sixth, Ninth Hour), and Prayer of the Twelfth Hour all have praises as a very important element; the worshipper says these praises from the heart. This is what the Agpia teaches us.

Additionally, there is glorification, rejoicing, and spiritual songs.

 * We begin the Midnight Prayer by saying: "Rise children of light, praise the Lord of hosts". We say to the Lord "Give us alertness, so we may learn how to stand before You at the time of prayer and send up to You appropriate glorification". We, then, sing Psalm 134(133) "Behold, bless the Lord, all you servants of the Lord, who by night stand in the house of the Lord! Lift up your hands in the sanctuary, and bless the Lord".

 * It is an invitation to praise that we repeat in the Prayer of the Twelfth Hour. We repeat this invitation in Psalm 113(112) of the Prayer of the Ninth Hour and the Morning Prayer; we say "Praise the Lord! Praise the Lord, O servants of the Lord, praise the name of the Lord". We also say, "Blessed be the name of the Lord from this time

forth and forevermore", and "From the rising of the sun to its going down the Lord's name is to be praised".

The worshipper sings of the beautiful characteristics of God in this praise; s/he says "The Lord is high above all the nations, and His glory above the heavens", and "Who is like the Lord our God, who dwells on high, who humbles Himself to behold the things that are in the heavens and in the earth...".

 * We praise the Lord in passages, such as the Trisagion. Thus, we say at every Hour of the seven Hours of Prayers "Holy God, Holy Almighty, Holy immortal...", and "Holy, Holy, Holy, is the Lord of hosts. Heaven and earth are full of Your glory and honor". This part is taken from the praise of the seraphim that was revealed to Isaiah the prophet (Isa. 6).

Furthermore, we say, in Psalm 51(50) that is said every Hour, "O Lord, open my lips, and my mouth shall show forth Your praise".

One of the Psalms that indicates the necessity of continuous praises is Psalm 34(33), which we say in the Prayer of the Third Hour. We say "I will bless the Lord at all times; His praise shall continually be in my mouth". Then we say "My soul shall make its boast in the Lord; the humble shall hear of it and be glad. Oh, magnify the Lord with me...", and "Oh, taste and see that the Lord is good". In the Gloria, of the Morning Prayer, we say with continuous praises "I give You blessing daily, and praise Your Holy Name forever and ever", and "You alone are Holy. You alone are the most high".

All this was mentioned in general terms; let us return to the Prayers of the Hours in more detail.

Praises in the Agpia

THE MORNING PRAYER

We say in Psalm 13(12) "My heart shall rejoice in Your salvation. I will sing to the Lord, because He has dealt bountifully with me". We also say in Psalm 16(15) "I will bless the Lord who has given me counsel". This is followed by gladness and rejoicing; we say "Therefore my heart is glad, and my glory rejoices". Moreover, we say in Psalm 27(26) "Therefore I will offer sacrifices of joy in His tabernacle; I will sing, yes, I will sing praises to the Lord". In Psalm 63(62), we say "When I remember You on my bed, I meditate on You in the night watches. Because You have been my help...".

One of the famous passages of praises in the Agpia is the Gloria. We say "Let us sing with the angels: Glory to God in the highest, peace on earth and goodwill towards men. We praise You, we bless You, we serve You, we worship You, we confess to You, we proclaim Your glory, and we thank You, for Your great glory...".

Furthermore, we say in the passages of the Morning Prayer "Let the senses and thoughts of light shine upon us...that we may deeply praise You with David, saying: My eyes are awake through the night, that I may meditate on Your word"

In the Absolution of the Morning Prayer, which we also say at the end of each Hour, we praise God for His wonderful characteristics and His attitude toward mankind. We say "For You are always worshipped and glorified in heaven and earth. O Christ, our good Lord, plenteous in patience, mercy and compassion, who loves the just and shows mercy to all sinners amongst whom I am the first. Who does not wish death for the sinner but repentance and life, calling us all to salvation for the promised forthcoming rewards".

Praying the Agpia

In another two absolutions in the Morning Prayer, we say "O Lord, God of hosts, existing before the ages and abiding forever, who created the sun to light up the day, and the night to provide rest for all people...", and "O giver of light, who makes the sun shine upon the righteous and the wicked; who created and gave light to the world..."

Contemplating the beautiful characteristics of God is considered to be praise. It strengthens faith as well as the relationship of the worshipper with God; the Agpia gets us used to this. We might not have such contemplation in our own, improvised prayer: we might only thank God or ask Him for something in improvised prayers.

> *Contemplating the beautiful characteristics of God is considered to be praise. It strengthens faith as well as the relationship of the worshipper with God*

PRAYER OF THE THIRD HOUR

We notice that praise is mixed with glorification. In Psalm 24(23), the worshipper says "The earth is the Lord's, and all its fullness, the world and those who dwell therein. For He has founded it upon the seas, and established it upon the waters". S/he says "Lift up your heads, O you gates! And the King of glory shall come in. Who is this King of glory? The Lord strong and mighty, the Lord mighty in battle...The Lord of hosts, He is the King of glory".

We also see that praise is accompanied by rejoicing due to the glory of God as well as His works. In Psalm 47(46), the worshipper says, "Oh, clap your hands, all you peoples! Shout to God with the voice of triumph! For the Lord Most High is awesome; He is a great King over the earth", and "God has gone up with a trumpet. Sing praises to God;

Praises in the Agpia

sing praises! Sing praises to our King; sing praises! For God is the King of all the earth...".

Praise is also related to the Lord's altar. In Psalm 26(25), the worshipper says "I will wash my hands in innocence; so I will go about Your altar, O Lord, that I may proclaim with the voice of thanksgiving, and tell of all Your wondrous works". Furthermore the worshipper says, in Psalm 29(28), "In His temple everyone says 'glory'".

In Psalm 43(42), the worshipper says "Oh, send out Your light and Your truth! Let them lead me; let them bring me to Your Holy hill and to Your tabernacle. Then I will go to the altar of God, to God my exceeding joy; and on the harp I will praise You, O God, my God...I shall yet praise Him, the help of my countenance and my God. Alleluia".

Regarding continuous praise, it is very clear in Psalm 34(33) what the worshipper desires "I will bless the Lord at all times; His praise shall continually be in my mouth...". We mentioned this previously.

PRAYER OF THE SIXTH HOUR

The worshipper praises God because He is just and merciful, as manifested on the cross.

Thus, the worshipper says in Psalm 85(84) "Surely His salvation is near to those who fear Him...Righteousness and peace have kissed each other. Truth shall spring out of the earth, and righteousness shall look down from heaven. Yes, the Lord will give what is good; and our land will yield its increase. Righteousness will go before Him, and shall make His footsteps our pathway".

In Psalm 57(56), the worshipper says "I will sing and give praise...Awake, lute and harp! I will awaken the dawn. I will praise You, O Lord, among the peoples; I will sing to You among the nations. For Your mercy reaches unto the heavens, and Your truth unto the clouds. Be exalted, O God, above the heavens; let Your glory be above all the earth. Alleluia".

In this Psalm we find mercy, righteousness, glory and exaltation of God, as we also find singing and praise, all are found together.

Furthermore, we find the glorification of God, due to the salvation that He offered, together with real gladness of the worshipper who says in Psalm 86(85) "All nations whom You have made shall come and worship Your name before You, O Lord, and shall glorify Your name. For You are great, and do wondrous things; You alone are God. Teach me Your way, O Lord; I will walk in Your truth; unite my heart to fear Your name. I will praise You, O Lord my God, with all my heart, and I will glorify Your name forevermore. For great is Your mercy toward me, and You have delivered my soul from the depths of Sheol".

The worshipper also praises the Lord for His Kingdom that started on the cross. This is found in Psalm 93(92), where the worshipper says "The Lord reigns, He is clothed with majesty; the Lord is clothed, He has girded Himself with strength. Surely the world is established, so that it cannot be moved", and "Holiness adorns Your house, O Lord, forever. Alleluia".

Moreover, the worshipper glorifies the Lord for His salvation in the passages of the Prayer of the Sixth Hour; s/he says "O Lord Christ, You gave salvation to the whole world when You spread Your undefiled hands on the cross, for this all nations give You praise saying: Glory be to You O' Lord". The worshipper also says "We were dead before, but we have been raised, and made worthy to inherit eternal life and to regain paradise, for this we thankfully glorify our immortal Lord Jesus".

Praises in the Agpia

PRAYER OF THE NINTH HOUR

Praise is frequent in the Psalms, so is talking about the Kingdom of God. Rejoicing is also frequent, for God defeated death by His death at this Hour. Thus, the worshipper starts Psalm 96(95) by saying "Oh, sing to the Lord a new song! Sing to the Lord, all the earth",

"Sing to the Lord, bless His name; proclaim the good news of His salvation from day to day", "Declare His glory among the nations, His wonders among all peoples",

"For the Lord is great and greatly to be praised; He is to be feared above all gods",

"Give to the Lord glory and strength. Give to the Lord the glory due to His name", and

"Say among the nations: the Lord reigns".

This praise is a new type of praise, because it is related to a new event through which the Lord reigned and was glorified. He offered to us salvation, which we should preach to all the peoples.

The worshipper repeats this praise in Psalm 98(97); s/he says "Oh, sing to the Lord a new song! For He has done marvelous things", and "The Lord has made known His salvation; His righteousness He has openly shown in the sight of the nations" The worshipper accompanies such praise with rejoicing saying, "All the ends of the earth have seen the salvation of our God. Shout joyfully to the Lord, all the earth; break forth in song, rejoice, and sing praises. Sing to the Lord with the harp, with the harp and the sound of a psalm, with trumpets and the sound of a horn; shout joyfully before the Lord, the King".

Rejoicing at this salvation is repeated in other Psalms. In Psalm 100(99), we say "Make a joyful shout to the Lord, all you lands! Serve the Lord with gladness; come before His presence with singing", and "Enter into His gates with thanksgiving, and into His courts with praise. Be thankful to Him, and bless His name. For the Lord is good; His mercy is everlasting...Alleluia".

In Psalm 97(96), the worshipper says "The Lord reigns; let the earth rejoice; let the multitude of isles be glad", "The heavens declare His righteousness, and all the peoples see His glory", "Worship Him, all you gods" and "Light is sown for the righteous, and gladness for the upright in heart. Rejoice in the Lord, You righteous, and give thanks at the remembrance of His holy name".

The feeling that the Hour of the death of our Lord is an Hour of glorification, rejoicing and gladness is a wonderful and deep feeling, for the Lord has reigned.

We glorify the Lord for He has defeated Satan; He has defeated death by His death and granted salvation to the whole world. He was mighty is His death, mighty in His love, and mighty in His salvation that is offered to the world.

We mention all of this in the Agpia Prayers. We may mention this in our own improvised prayers, but it is unlikely that we do so in a detailed fashion as in the Agpia Prayers.

Salvation in the Agpia Prayers

Salvation is a principal topic in the Agpia Prayers. We always ask to be saved and we thank God for this salvation. We mention the Lord's salvation and His redemption in every Hour of the Agpia.

 * Reciting the Creed, that is common to Prayers, we say "He descended from heaven for us and for our salvation, and was incarnated from the Holy Spirit and of the Virgin Mary, and became man. He was crucified for us at the time of Pontius Pilate. He suffered and was buried; arose from the dead...".

 * We say in the Trisagion "Who was crucified for our sake, have mercy on us".

 * We also say to St Virgin Mary, in the introduction of the Creed, "...for you gave birth to the Savior of the world. He came and saved our souls". Furthermore, we say to her, in the passages of the Morning Prayer "May you ask Him to redeem the world He has created...".

Praying the Agpia

* In the Thanksgiving Prayer, we say "our Lord God and Savior, Jesus Christ". Thus, we do not only mention His divinity, but also His salvation. These titles are repeated a lot in the Agpia Prayers...

* In the concluding Prayer that we say at the end of each Agpia Prayer, we say "Who does not wish death for the sinner but repentance and life, calling us all to salvation for the promised forthcoming rewards".

The Lord's salvation through redeeming us is present before out eyes every day and every Hour. Yet, it is more extensive in the Prayer of the Sixth Hour of the day.

In the passages of this Prayer, we say to the Lord "O' Lord Christ, You gave salvation to the whole world when You spread Your undefiled hands on the cross, for this all nations give You praise saying; 'Glory be to You O' Lord". In the following passage, we say "...for You were pleased to willingly go to the cross to rescue Your creation from the slavery of the enemy", and "We thank You Christ, for You filled us all with joy, when You came to help the world, glory be to You".

This is why we call Him "Savior", experiencing joy through His cross, and seeing His glory on that same cross.

We say to St Virgin Mary "through the cross of your Son, Hades has fallen and death destroyed. We were dead before, but we have been raised, and made worthy to inherit eternal life and to regain paradise, for this we thankfully glorify our immortal Lord Jesus".

Thus, we feel that the Lord's salvation that was for our sake deserves glorification and thanksgiving. This salvation shows the Lord's power.

Salvation in the Agpia Prayers

We acknowledge that through this salvation we were moved from death to life; this salvation opened to us the gate of Paradise and saved us from Hades. We know that the Cross was there because of the sin that Adam and Eve dared to commit in Paradise. We say "Lord, who on the Sixth day, at the Sixth hour You were nailed to the Cross for the sin that Adam dared to commit in Paradise...".

In our Prayers, we remember the works of the Cross as well as the consequences; we say "O' Jesus Christ, our God, who was nailed to the Cross at the sixth hour. You mortified sin by the Cross, by Your death You raised the dead; that is man, who was dead in sin". Indeed, praying with the Agpia is full of doctrines and theological issues. This is the depth of Prayers, they are not just superficial words.

Furthermore, in the passages of the Prayer of the Sixth Hour, we talk to St Virgin Mary saying about the Lord that "He to whom you gave birth is the merciful redeemer. He suffered to rescue us". Therefore, we supplicate to Him saying "Help us for the sake of Your glory, God save us and forgive our sins for the sake of Your Holy name". We also thank God the Father who so loved the world that He gave His only begotten Son, that whoever believes in Him should not perish but have everlasting life (John 3:16).

Accordingly, we say in the Absolution of the Prayer of the Sixth Hour, "We give thanks to You, our Almighty King, Father of our Lord and Savior Jesus Christ, and we glorify You for You have made the hour of suffering of Your Only Begotten Son a time of prayer and comfort".

Thus, we thank, praise and glorify the Lord, and we, indeed, rejoice because of His salvation and Cross. In Psalm 118(117) of the Sunset Prayer, we say "The Lord is my strength and song, and He has become my salvation". We repeat this sentence of the Psalm a lot during the Passion Week, as we focus our emotions on the pains of the Lord and on the salvation that He offered to the world.

The Lord's salvation is not only mentioned in the Prayer of the Sixth Hour, but is mentioned continually. We will try to follow this in the Agpia Prayers.

THE MORNING PRAYER

In Psalm 13(12), we say, "My heart shall rejoice in Your salvation. I will sing to the Lord, because He has dealt bountifully with me". Thus, we acknowledge that the Lord's salvation is the source of gladness, praise, singing, and rejoicing. We also say in Psalm 70(69) "Let all those who seek You rejoice and be glad in You; and let those who love Your salvation say continually: Let God be magnified".

Therefore, we magnify the Lord for this salvation that He offered to mankind. We magnify Him all the time because this salvation was great for the Lord saved everyone from the trap of death; He defeated death by His death. He is the Lord whose words in Psalm 12(11) we repeat in the Morning Prayer "For the oppression of the poor, for the sighing of the needy, now I will arise, says the Lord, I will set him in the safety for which he yearns". This is why we say to Him, in the same Psalm "Help, Lord, for the godly man ceases! For the faithful disappear from among the sons of men".

As we mention salvation in the Morning Prayer, we also mention it in the Prayer of the Third Hour.

PRAYER OF THE THIRD HOUR

The worshipper mentions this salvation in detail in Psalm 30(29) "O Lord, You have brought my soul up from the grave; You have kept me alive, that I should not go down to the pit". The worshipper, then, says "Sing praise

Salvation in the Agpia Prayers

to the Lord, You saints of His, and give thanks at the remembrance of His holy name". S/he starts the Psalm by saying, "I will extol You, O Lord".

In regards to thanksgiving for the deliverance from the grave (Hades), this is a repeated theme in the same Psalm (30(29)). In a conversation with God, the worshipper says "What profit is there in my blood, when I go down to the pit? Will the dust praise You"? As a result, s/he thanks the Lord afterwards saying "Hear, O Lord, and have mercy on me".

This scenario is also found in Psalm 86(85) of the Prayer of the Sixth Hour "I will praise You, O Lord my God, with all my heart, and I will glorify Your name forevermore. For great is Your mercy toward me", and "You have delivered my soul from the depths of Sheol". Indeed, this deliverance from Sheol (Hades) is salvation that was achieved on the Cross.

The worshipper asks for the same thing in the Prayer of the Ninth Hour; s/he says to the Lord "Shine unto us the light, which You gave to those who were in the darkness of Hades. Restore us all to Paradise". Thus, the worshipper remembers that through the salvation that the Lord offered to her/him on the Cross, He shone light on those who were in the darkness of Hades, and that He restored them to the Paradise of Joy.

This great salvation is also mentioned in Psalm 29(28) in the Prayer of the Third Hour; the worshipper talks about the power of the Lord saying "The voice of the Lord is powerful; the voice of the Lord is full of majesty". Further, s/he says, "The voice of the Lord divides the flames of fire. The voice of the Lord shakes the wilderness", and "The Lord sits as King forever. The Lord will give strength to His people". The worshipper also says in Psalm 34(33)

"This poor man cried out, and the Lord heard him, and saved him out of all his troubles", and "The Lord is near to those who have a broken heart, and saves such as have a contrite spirit".

In the passages of the Prayer of the Third Hour, we supplicate to the Holy Spirit to purify and save us. We say "We ask You to graciously come and dwell within us, purify us from iniquity and save our souls". We also ask for salvation from the Son, the Savior; we say "Lord, abide with us as You did with the apostles when You gave them Your peace, we ask You to grant us Your peace, our Savior; save us and spare our souls".

PRAYER OF THE SIXTH HOUR

Our elaborated talk about the Lord's salvation is obvious in the passages and Absolution of this Prayer. Furthermore, we start the Prayer with Psalm 54(53) saying "Save me, O God, by Your name". We also say in Psalm 57(56) "He shall send from heaven and save me, He reproaches the one who would swallow me up". Whom did God send from heaven except the Son, the Savior?! The worshipper also says "God shall send forth His mercy and truth: my soul is among lions" (Ps. 57(56)).

Perhaps one of the most obvious Psalms about salvation in this Hour's Prayer is Psalm 85(84); the worshipper says "Restore us, O God of our salvation, and cause Your anger toward us to cease". Moreover, s/he says in the same psalm "Will You not revive us again, that Your people may rejoice in You?", and "Show us Your mercy, O Lord, and grant us Your salvation". Immediately, the worshipper feels God's answer, so s/he says "I will hear what God the Lord will speak, for He will speak peace to His people and to His saints; but let them not turn back to folly", and "Surely His salvation is near to those who fear Him".

Salvation in the Agpia Prayers

Then, the worshipper explains the salvation that was on the Cross, which showed that God's justice and mercy are united. Thus, s/he says "Mercy and truth have met together; righteousness and peace have kissed each other".

PRAYER OF THE NINTH HOUR

How beautiful it is what is said in this Prayer about the right thief, as a first fruit of our salvation. We sing in the Prayer saying "O Righteous Lord who received the confession of the thief on the cross, accept us who deserve the judgement of death because of our sins" and "With him we acknowledge our sins, confessing Your divinity saying: Lord remember us when You come into Your kingdom".

We mention the work of the Lord, so we call Him saying "O' Righteous Lord, with Your death You defeated death, with Your resurrection You made eternal life manifest", and "The world rejoices at the acceptance of salvation...".

We say to God the Father in the Absolution of this Prayer "Grant us to be worthy of Your calling and when we are released from this body, may we be counted among those who kneel before Your throne and are worthy of the sufferings of Your Only Begotten Son, our Lord Jesus Christ. Grant us Your mercy, forgive us our sins and save us with the hosts of saints...".

One of the most beautiful verses in Psalm 96(95), the first Psalm in the Prayer of the Ninth Hour, is "Proclaim the good news of His salvation from day to day". Through this salvation the Kingdom of the Lord began. This is why the statement "The Lord reigns" is repeated in the Psalms of the Prayer of the Ninth Hour; examples include Psalm 97(96) and Psalm 99(98). Talking about the Lord's sitting at the right hand of the Father is also repeated; for example, in Psalm 110(109). Praising the Lord for this salvation is repeated often and is manifested by the statement "Oh, sing to the Lord a new song".

Gladness and rejoicing in the Lord's salvation is felt a lot in this Prayer. Examples include "Rejoice in the Lord, you righteous" (Ps. 97(96)), and "Light is sown for the righteous, and gladness for the upright in heart" (Ps. 97(96)). The worshipper says "The Lord has made known His salvation; His righteousness He has openly sown in the sight of the nations" (Ps. 98(97)). S/he also says, in the same Psalm "All the ends of the earth have seen the salvation of our God".

Thus, the worshipper asks everyone to praise, rejoice and sing; s/he says "Sing to the Lord with the harp, with the harp and the sound of a psalm, with trumpets and the sound of a horn. Sing to the Lord with the harp" (Ps. 98(97)). Then, s/he states the reason "He has sent redemption to His people" (Ps. 111(110)).

As a consequence of all of this, the worshipper rejoices in the Lord's salvation; s/he says in Psalm 116:10-19(115) "I will take up the cup of salvation, and call upon the name of the Lord". The worshipper is glad with death, because it is not death anymore, but rather "Precious in the sight of the Lord is the death of His saints" (Ps. 116:10-19(115)). This is why the worshipper says "Return to Your rest, O my soul, for the Lord has dealt bountifully with You. For You have delivered my soul from death, my eyes from tears, and my feet from falling. I will walk before the Lord in the land of the living. Alleluia".

The Sunset Prayer

The worshipper says in Psalm 118(117) "I will praise You, for You have answered me, and have become my salvation", "This is the day which the Lord has made; we will rejoice and be glad in it", and "The right hand of the Lord does

Salvation in the Agpia Prayers

valiantly. I shall not die, but live". Why? Because the Lord has died on my behalf. Thus, "The voice of rejoicing and salvation is in the tents of the righteous" (Ps. 118(117)). Through salvation, the gate of Paradise was opened. As a consequence, the worshipper says, "This is the gate of the Lord, through which the righteous shall enter" (Ps. 118(117)). Furthermore, during the worshipper's gladness caused by the Lord's salvation, s/he says "The Lord has done great things for us, whereof we are glad" (Ps. 126(125)).

The worshipper, thus, prays in the passages of the Sunset Prayer saying, "Take me now, my Savior into Your Fatherly embrace". Also, s/he says "Count me among those of the eleventh hour".

PRAYER OF THE TWELFTH HOUR

The worshipper says in one of the passages "Have mercy upon me and save my soul", and "save me Lord, for I am seeking You". Then, s/he prays asking her/his soul to be prepared before the time is too late, and to repent in order to be saved.

In the first Psalm of this Prayer (130(129)), the worshipper says "With the Lord there is mercy, and with Him". S/he also says in Psalm 142(141) "You are my refuge, my portion in the land of the living", and "Bring my soul out of prison". Furthermore, in the Gospel of this Prayer, the worshipper remembers Simeon the elderly; "...because my eyes have seen Your salvation" (Luke 2:30).

It is really obvious that salvation is an essential element in all the Prayers of the Hours in the Agpia, including Psalms, passages, and Absolutions, and also in this passage of the Gospel...

Praying the Agpia

THE MIDNIGHT PRAYER

It is enough that this Prayer begins with statements about salvation; the worshipper says "Rise children of light, praise the Lord of hosts, may he bestow upon us the salvation of our souls".

Also, s/he says "Let God rise, and all His enemies will scatter and those who despise His Holy name will disappear. As for Your people may they multiply through Your blessing thousands performing Your will".

Furthermore, Psalm 119(118) (the Great Psalm) is full of verses about salvation:

* "Let Your mercy come also to me, O Lord, Your salvation according to Your word"

* "My soul faints for Your salvation, but I hope in Your word"

* "I am Yours, save me; for I have sought Your precepts"

* "Hold me up, and I shall be safe"

* "My eyes fail from seeking Your salvation"

* "Salvation is far from the wicked, for they do not seek Your statutes"

* "Lord, I hope for Your salvation, and I do Your commandments"

* "Let Your hand become my help"

* "I long for Your salvation, O Lord, and Your law is my delight"

We notice in all of these Prayers that salvation is closely linked to the commandments of God.

The Agpia, Knowing the Way, and our Spiritualities are Gifts of God

KNOWING THE WAY

The worshipper who uses the Agpia asks God to show her/him the way and to teach her/him His will. S/he also asks God to guide and strengthen her/him in such a way and path.

The worshipper says in Psalm 25(24), of the Morning Prayer, "Show me Your ways, O Lord; teach me Your paths", and "Lead me in Your truth and teach me, for You are the God of my salvation". The worshipper also says in the same Psalm "Good and upright is the Lord; therefore He teaches sinners in the way", and "The humble He guides in justice, and the humble He teaches His way".

In Psalm 27(26), the worshipper says "Teach me Your way, O Lord, and lead me in a smooth path". Furthermore, s/he says in Psalm 143(142) of the Morning Prayer "Cause me to know the way in which I should walk, for I lift up my soul to You", "Your Spirit is good. Lead me in the land of uprighteousness", and "Teach me to do Your will, for You are my Lord".

Indeed, who remembers, everyday, to ask God to teach her/him the way and guide her/him in it?! Who asks God to lead her/him in the upright and smooth path, everyday?! Who asks God, everyday, to teach her/him to do His will?! Who asks for all of these things everyday except the worshipper who uses the Agpia? Everyone says that they know the way of God! However, it is good that the worshipper who uses the Agpia asks for the guidance of the Holy Spirit.

In addition to knowing the way, we say in the Absolution of the Morning Prayer "We ask You O' Lord Master of all, to enlighten our minds, hearts and understanding". Moreover, we say everyday, in the passages of the Morning Prayer, "Let the senses and the thoughts of the light shine upon us, and let us not be covered by the darkness of pain that we may deeply praise You with David, saying: My eyes are awake through the night, that I my meditate on Your word".

We say in the Absolution of the Prayer of the Ninth Hour "Shine unto us the light which You gave to those who were in the darkness of Hades. Restore us all to Paradise...". Furthermore, we say in the introduction of the Midnight Prayer "When we stand up bodily before You, take away from us the sleep of carelessness, and give us alertness, so we may learn how to stand before You at the time of prayer and send up to You appropriate glorification to gain forgiveness of our sins". As we ask the Lord to give us alertness, we also ask Him to give us all our spiritual life.

There are many other requests that we say in the Great Psalm (119(118)):

"I am a stranger in the earth"

Gifts of God

"Open my eyes, that I may see wondrous things from Your law"

"You are good, and do good; teach me Your statutes"

"Deal with Your servant according to Your mercy, and teach me Your statutes"

"I am Your servant; give me understanding, that I may know Your testimonies"

"Make Your face shine upon Your servant, and teach me Your statutes"

It is, indeed, good for the worshipper to ask God for knowledge, through which s/he recognizes the way that leads to God.

Our Spiritualities are a Gift from God

In the Agpia Prayers, we do not acknowledge an ability that we have, but rather we ask God to help us; we ask Him to grant us what He requires from us. Thus, we say in the Thanksgiving Prayer at the beginning of each Agpia Prayer "We ask You and appeal to Your goodness O Lover of mankind that You grant us to conclude this blessed day and all the days of our life in peace and in Your fear". We do not promise God or make a vow that we are going to behave in a good manner this day, but rather we say "grant us...".

We do not say this only at the beginning of the Prayer, but also in the Absolution of the Morning Prayer, with the same meaning and same spirit. We say "Grant us to please You this present day". Indeed, how beautiful and deep this request is. How obvious humility is in it... You, O' Lord, want us to please You in this new day that You granted us. But we can do nothing without You, O' Lord (John15: 5).

Therefore, "Grant us to please You this present day"... You grant it, O' Lord, not an ability that we have that grants it.

The worshipper, then, continues her/his request by saying to the Lord "Protect us from every evil, every sin and every enemy". It is the same request that the worshipper says at the end of the Thanksgiving Prayer: "all envy, all temptation, all works of Satan, all intrigues of the wicked; rising up of enemies, seen and unseen; do cast away from us and all Your people, and from this Holy place".

These are the same requests, but in a more detailed fashion. They are also said at the conclusion of every Agpia Prayer, with more details: "Ease our lives, and guide us to act according to Your commandments".

Furthermore, this is what we say in the Absolution of the Prayer of the Third Hour: "Lead us to a spiritual life so that we may seek righteousness and make us worthy to serve You in purity and goodness". It is a request from God "Lead us to a spiritual life".

Almost the same request is made in the Absolution of the Prayer of the Sixth Hour, where we say "Lord grant us an unblemished life of peace and goodness to please Your Holy and Glorified name". This gift that we ask God to grant us is almost what we ask for in the Absolution of the Prayer of the Ninth Hour: "We ask You, in His blessed and glorious name, to raise our minds above worldly care and bodily desires to the remembrance of Your heavenly commandments". Furthermore, we say "Grant us to be worthy of Your calling", and "Lord cast away from us the power of the adversary and his evil hosts".

In the passages of the Prayer of the Ninth Hour, the worshipper says "Mortify our carnal senses, O' Christ our God, and deliver us"; s/he also says "Sanctify my soul, enlighten my mind and let me partake of the grace of Your

Gifts of God

life giving sacraments", and "Lord remember us when You come into Your Kingdom".

Similarly, in the Absolution of the Sunset Prayer, the worshipper says "Save us from the temptations of the enemy and defeat all his traps set against us". The worshipper also says "In this coming night, give us peace without pain or anxiety or fatigue or illusion so we may pass through the night in peace and chastity and awake to praise You and pray to You".

Almost the same request is made in the Absolution of the Prayer of the Twelfth Hour "Grant us a peaceful night and give us a sleep free of all anxiety, send us the guardian angel to protect us from every evil, temptation or the strike of the enemy". And just before this request, the worshipper would have said "Lord, by Your grace protect us this night from sin".

It is a lesson that the Agpia offers us: to ask God to grant us a holy life.

www.ingramcontent.com/pod-product-compliance
Lightning Source LLC
LaVergne TN
LVHW041300080426
835510LV00009B/817